Editor
Amy Gammill, M. Ed.

Editorial Project Manager
Elizabeth Morris, Ph.D.

Editor-in-Chief
Sharon Coan, M.S. Ed.

Cover Artist
Lesley Palmer

Art Coordinator
Kevin Barnes

Art Director
CJae Froshay

Imaging
Alfred Lau

Product Manager
Phil Garcia

Acknowledgements
Microsoft Office© is 1991-2003
Microsoft Corporation. All rights
reserved. *Microsoft PowerPoint* is a
trademark of Microsoft Corporation,
registered in the U.S. and other
countries.

Publisher
Mary D. Smith, M.S. Ed.

Author

Midge Frazel

Teacher Created Resources, Inc.
6421 Industry Way
Westminster, CA 92683
www.teachercreated.com
ISBN-0-7439-3816-X
©2003 Teacher Created Resources, Inc.
Reprinted, 2005
Made in U.S.A.

Table of Contents

Introduction

If you've taken a basic workshop—or explored *Microsoft PowerPoint* on your own—and can now construct a simple presentation, then it is time make your presentations and slide shows into something really special. Step up to another level by learning some simple tricks that will make your presentations look professionally created. At the same time gather some tips to make it all a little easier.

The tips and tricks in this book are aimed at educators who are preparing to use *PowerPoint* as a teaching tool or as a productivity tool for their students. No matter what your subject or grade level, use *PowerPoint* to improve the delivery of your curriculum content. In addition, by using *PowerPoint* you can motivate and model the use of technology in the classroom. Whether you are using *PowerPoint* to present information to students for note-taking, or as a one-computer tutorial for delivery of content to enhance student instruction, this book offers ideas and shortcuts to save time in preparing and delivering instructional material.

Today's students are motivated to learn in different ways than previous generations of learners. As a multimedia instruction tool, *PowerPoint* can help teachers cover material quickly and easily in a medium suited to this technologically-oriented generation.

If you are a teacher who uses *PowerPoint* on both Windows and Macintosh computers, this book is an excellent cross-platform resource. It has been divided into two sections, one for Mac users and the other Windows users of *PowerPoint*. The Macintosh section has been prepared for presentations created with *PowerPoint* 2001 (part of *Office 2001*). If you are using Office: mac v X on your computer, the same instructions will apply. The interface will appear on your screen looking just a bit differently than the screenshots in this book. If you have an earlier version of *PowerPoint*, many of these tips and tricks will still work for you. These instructions can be found on pages 1-44 of this side of the book.

If you flip the book over, you will find the Windows instructions for *Tips and Tricks for Using Microsoft PowerPoint*. The Windows section has been prepared for presentations created with *PowerPoint 2000* (part of Office 2000) and *PowerPoint 2002* (part of Office XP).

The author of this book has a resource page for *PowerPoint* users located at
http://www.midgefrazel.net/powerpoint.html
It is filled with links to current Web resources such as tutorials and multimedia resources appropriate for classroom use.

So, power on your computer, start *PowerPoint*, and start reading!

Slide Creation Time Savers

Planning and developing each slide in a presentation takes the largest amount of time. Writing and editing the content and planning the delivery are the bulk of the work of presentation design. In this section you will find some timesaving ideas for basic slide creation.

 Tip: Detour Ahead!

Create your title slide first, and then decide on one of the slide layouts for the majority of the rest of your slides. Create several slides with that layout before you add content. You can always change the slide layout later or even delete unneeded slides. Having the slides ready will make adding and editing your content faster.

To quickly create a new slide with the same layout as the one chosen previously, follow the instructions below:

PowerPoint 2001 users can hold down the **Shift** key on the keyboard while clicking the **New Slide** icon on the **Standard** toolbar.

 Tip: Where's the Project Gallery? (OS X users refer to page 37)

When PowerPoint 2001 is first launched, the Project Gallery appears with the PowerPoint Presentation project icon selected and with a choice of a Category for a Blank Document. Most users simply click the OK button, which closes this Gallery. To make it reappear, click the **File** menu and choose **Project Gallery**. To disable the Project Gallery from showing at startup, select **Do Not Show at Startup**.

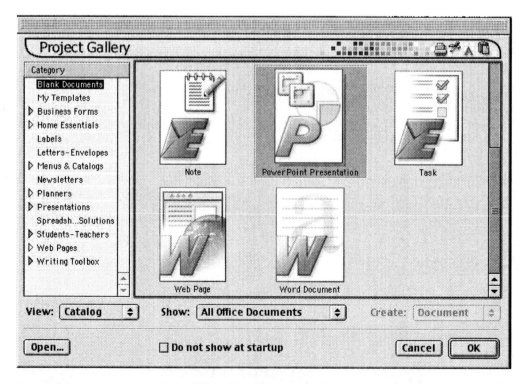

Tip: Selecting is Imperative

It can't be emphasized enough that items placed on *PowerPoint* slides must be selected in order to make changes to them. Most of the time, you can tell if something is selected by the appearance of selection handles. If you are struggling to manipulate something on a slide, check to see if the object is selected. If not, click on the object to select it and try again.

Selection handle

 ## Tip: Formatting Palette

PowerPoint 2001 has a handy floating Formatting Palette that is ready for you to use at any time. It floats on the right side of the screen. If it is not visible, click the **View** menu and choose **Formatting Palette**. For even quicker access, click the **Formatting Palette** button on the **Standard** toolbar. This palette displays different formatting features depending upon the objects with which you are working.

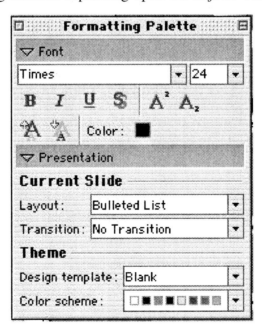

Tip: Adjusting the Panes

If you like creating your slides in Normal view so that you can work on the current slide, the outline, and notes all at once, then learn to adjust the size of these panes to increase or decrease each one as needed. Place your cursor over the heavy line (called the splitter bar) located between panes. The cursor should transform into a hollow box with arrows. When you see this cursor, simply click and hold, then drag to resize the pane.

 ## Trick: Putting Panes Back to Normal

If you are sharing a computer with others or are responsible for a group of computers in a classroom, library, or lab setting, it is inevitable that users will resize the panes and create a maintenance headache. Users of *PowerPoint* 2001 can resize the panes to the default setting by pressing the **Shift** key and clicking the **Normal View** button.

 ## Tip: Change the Bullets

The Slide AutoLayouts that contain bulleted text allow for quick entry of important text and phrases. Jazz them up by changing the way the bullets appear on your slide. First, on a bulleted slide, click within the typed bulleted text. From the **Format** menu, choose **Bullets and Numbering**. In the **Bullets and Numbering** dialog box, click the **Bulleted** tab. Examine the available styles, click on one to choose it, and then click **OK**.

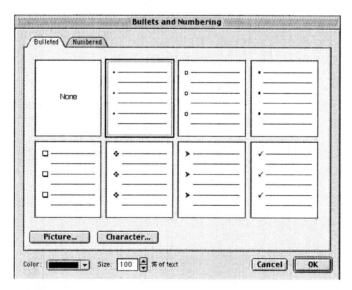

 ## Trick: Tricky Bullets

If the sample styles for the bulleted text aren't fancy enough, you can change them to tiny "pictures" instead. Customized bullets (often called characters) are made from special symbols in a font. In the **Bullets and Numbering** dialog box with the **Bulleted** tab selected, click on the button labeled **Customize or Character**. In the next dialog box, use the **Font** drop down list to choose an installed font.

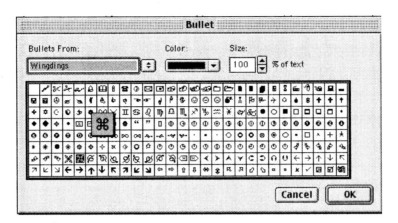

You can also use your own graphic as a bullet. Of course, the graphic must be very small in size and stored on your hard drive. If you have one you'd like to use, click the **Picture** button to open it.

 ## Tip: Duplicate Your Favorite Slide

You might be tempted to copy and paste objects from one slide to another but it is easier to duplicate an entire slide and then eliminate or edit the objects on it. Why work so hard? To do this, select the slide, click the **Insert** menu, and choose **Duplicate Slide**. An exact copy of the entire slide will be inserted.

 ## Trick: Picture Backgrounds (OS X refer to page 39)

Your students will enjoy using digital photographs for their reports. To add digital images as a background for the slides, click the **Format** menu and choose **Background**. Next, click the drop-down box and choose **Fill Effects**.

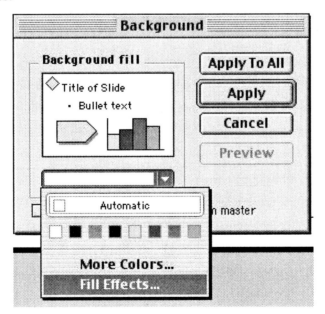

Then click the **Select Picture** button and navigate to the location where your images are stored. Select the image you desire and it will appear (along with its filename), as will a sample of how it will look on your slide. Click **OK** to choose the image. The **Background** dialog box appears again to confirm your choice. Click the **Apply** button to add the image to the slide.

Tip: Background Check

You can also fill the background of your slides with a solid color, shaded gradient, or a texture. Click the **Format** menu and choose **Background**. In the **Background** dialog box, choose a color, **More Colors**, or **Fill Effects**. When using Fill Effects, experiment with the choices in each tabbed section. Remember, your background, text colors, and graphics have to work nicely together so think carefully before using an orange plaid texture as a filled background!

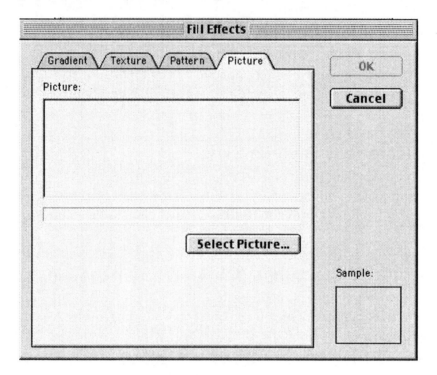

Idea: Digital Image Title Slides

Digital images from your school field trips make excellent title slides for multimedia reports that summarize class experiences. Since text is hard to read on highly colored backgrounds, change the text to a complementary light color for easy readability. (Photograph taken by Kathleen Wasik, fourth grade teacher, Hull, Massachusetts.)

Trick: Blank is Good

After designing your title slide, try creating the rest of your slides with the blank (white) background. As you place images or drawn objects on your slides, you may discover that a highly colored background will detract from your message and may make your text unreadable from a distance. Concentrate on the purpose of your presentation. You can always add a background or a design template to your slides after you have created them.

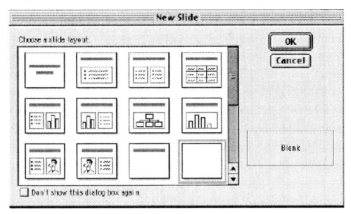

Tip: Selecting Slides in Slide Sorter View

Experienced *PowerPoint* users know that the easiest way to view and select multiple slides is by using the Slide Sorter view. To select multiple slides, first click the **View** menu and choose **Slide Sorter** or click the **Slide Sorter View** icon in the **Views** area. Then click the **Edit** menu and choose **Select All**. Remember, slides that have been selected have a heavy border around them in Slide Sorter view. To deselect slides, simply click in the white area between slides.

Often you may need to select just a group of slides. Select consecutive or adjacent slides by holding down the **Command** key while clicking the beginning and ending slide. All the slides between them will be selected. To select non-adjacent slides, hold down the **Shift** key and click each slide. Below, non-consecutive slides (2, 4, 9, and 12) have been selected.

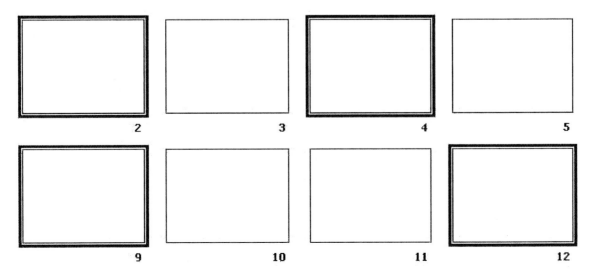

Trick: Save the Fonts

If you are fond of using exotic fonts for the text on your slides, remember that they may not be present on the computer you will use to show your presentation. Some fonts, like Times New Roman or Arial, can be found on most computers. This is why these are the default fonts in a new presentation.

Remember, use caution when picking a fancy font. The font you choose will need to be readable at a distance. Keep in mind that special fonts can be purchased for typing math and science equations and foreign languages.

 Tip: Font Substitution

If you wish to replace one font with another throughout a presentation, first choose **Format** then **Replace Fonts**. In the **Replace:** field, select the font you wish to change and in the **With:** field, choose the new font you wish to use. Click **Replace**. Repeat this procedure to replace other fonts. This tip can come in handy if you forgot to embed your fonts in the presentation and have to substitute other ones in a hurry!

 Tip: Special Ways with Fonts

Although many formatting changes can be accomplished quickly and easily using the handy Formatting palette, you may choose to use the Font dialog box to apply special formatting to selected text on your slides. For example, you may need to use superscript or subscript. Select the text that needs to be formatted, then click the **Format** menu and choose **Font**. Choose the effect you want. To see how it will look on your slide, click the **Preview** button before clicking **OK**. Although fancy fonts may be fun, consider how they will look during a presentation or in the handouts of your slides.

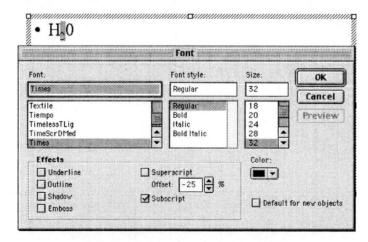

Trick: Don't Underline!

The Font dialog box contains an underline option that you shouldn't use routinely. If you are looking to underline text in a title placeholder, draw a line under it instead of using the underline feature. Underlining is a commonly used method to indicate a hyperlink; your audience may be confused by your underlined text and think it is a Web address (URL). Finally, the underlined text may be unreadable at a distance.

Don't Underline!

- yyyyyyy
- Underlined text can be difficult to read.

 ## Tip: Use Format Painter

Save yourself a lot of time by learning about the Format Painter feature. The job of this tool is to copy all of the formatting (font style, size, bold, color, effects, etc.) of selected text and quickly apply it to other text on the same slide or on other slides in your presentation. You can also use Format Painter to copy carefully applied formatting from one object to other objects.

To use Format Painter with text, first apply your desired formatting to the text in your title or body text placeholders. Then select the text and click the **Format Painter** icon on the **Standard** toolbar. The cursor will change to a paintbrush. Place the paintbrush on the text to which you want to apply the formatting and click. Instantly, your text will be changed to the desired formatting.

Use Format Painter to apply the chosen effects to multiple text and objects by double-clicking the **Format Painter** icon and then using it to apply formatting in more than one place. Stop the Format Painter by pressing the **ESC** key on the keyboard.

 ## Tip: Get Around

Here are some useful keyboard shortcuts to move around within your presentation during the slide creation process. (Note: Make sure there are no placeholders or objects selected.)

- To move up one slide, press the **Up Arrow** key.
- To move down one slide, press the **Down Arrow** key.
- To move to the first slide, press the **Command** and **Home** keys.
- To move to the last slide, press the **Command** and **End** keys.

You can also move through a presentation by using the arrows on the keyboard or the scroll box on the scroll bar.

Useful and Easy PowerPoint Art

Not artistic? Use the Drawing toolbar to create very professional-looking effects in a matter of minutes (it's lots of fun, too!).

 Tip: Objects Are Everything

Experiment on a blank slide when learning to create art effects. Delete the slide when you are done and no one will see the result of your experimentation.

Things drawn on slides are called *objects* no matter what their size and shape. You manipulate objects when they are selected, that is, when the selection handles are showing.

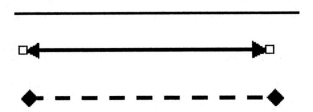

 Tip: Show the Drawing Toolbar

To create objects on your slides, you'll need to use the Drawing toolbar. If it is visible, it will most likely be on the right-hand side of the screen. If it isn't visible, turn it on by first selecting **Toolbars** from the **View** menu. A list of toolbars will appear. You will notice that the visible toolbars have checkmarks next to their names. Click the name of the toolbar you would like to have visible and a checkmark will appear. When you exit the menu, the toolbar will show up on your screen. Note that the Drawing toolbar may not be showing all of the available icons. Click the small downward-pointing arrow at the bottom of the toolbar to see more choices.

Tip: Straight Lines and Arrowheads

Draw straight lines on your *PowerPoint* slides easily by holding down the **Shift** key while dragging to create a new line. To change the line thickness, first click the **Line Style** icon on the **Drawing** toolbar. From the pop-up menu, choose a line size. To select a color for the line, click on the **Line Color** icon and choose a color. You can create dashed lines with the **Dash Style** icon.

Lines that have arrow ends are created the same way using the Arrow tool. First click on the **Arrow** icon and draw your line. With the arrow line selected, click on the **Arrow Style** tool and select a style from the list. If you need a straight arrow, hold down the **Shift** key while drawing. Arrow lines can also be colored by using the Line Color icon.

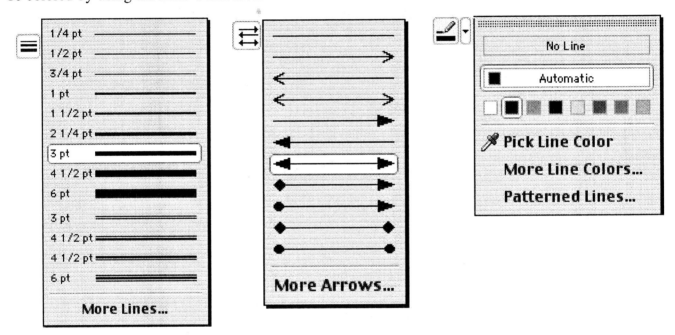

 ## Tip: Duplicate and Drag-Duplicate

Duplicate a line by selecting it, and then pressing **Command-D**.

Create a "Rip-off" of a selected object by holding down the **Option** key and dragging as if you were ripping the second copy away from the first. Once you get the hang of this technique you'll find a lot of uses for it. (This works with clip art and digital images too!)

 ## Trick: Multiple Attributes

It's fairly tedious and time-consuming to change multiple attributes on a single line or arrowhead, so try this trick. Select the line. Click the **Format** menu and choose **AutoShape**. Set all of the style and color options at once using this dialog box. (Note: This trick can be used with any object drawn with the Draw tools on the Drawing toolbar.)

Tip: Oval or Circle, Rectangle or Square

Next to the line and arrow tools on the Drawing Toolbar are the oval and rectangle tools. After drawing an oval or rectangle on your slide, select it and use the Format AutoShapes feature to set the outline width. To do this, in the **Format AutoShapes** dialog box, select the **Colors and Lines** tab, then choose **Fill Color**. Use the **No Fill** option to make the shape empty.

Create perfect circles instead of ovals by holding down the **Shift** key while drawing with the **Oval** tool. Make perfect squares by pressing the **Shift** key while drawing with the **Rectangle** tool.

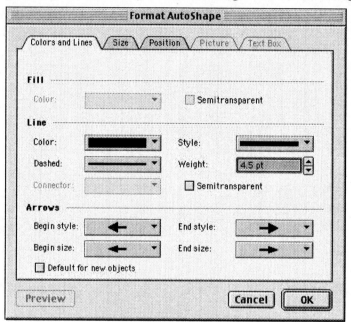

 Idea: Venn Diagram Graphic Organizer

On a blank slide, use the tips you just learned to create a circle with no fill. Select the circle and duplicate it. Drag the second circle to overlap the first, thus creating a Venn diagram. Select both circles with **Command-A**. On the **Drawing** toolbar, click the **Draw** icon, and from the fly-out menu choose **Align or Distribute**, and then **Align Top**.

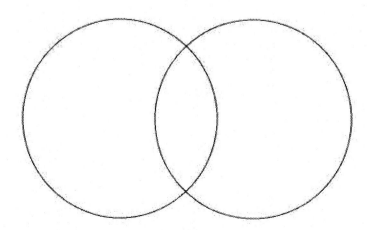

Putting Graphics to Work

Tip: AutoShapes Save Time

Instead of spending time looking for just the right graphic, take a look at the myriad of shapes that are available to you in the AutoShapes menu on the Drawing toolbar. (Remember, if you don't see the Drawing toolbar at the bottom of your screen, click the **View** menu, choose **Toolbars** and make sure there is a checkmark next to **Drawing**.) With the Drawing toolbar visible, click on **AutoShapes** to examine the categories of graphic objects like **Basic Shapes** and **Stars and Banners**. These useful shapes can be resized and reshaped to make dynamic objects for your slides.

Trick: Tear Off the Palette

Several menus on the Drawing toolbar can be ripped off from the toolbar to become floating palettes. Palettes can be placed alongside your slides for quick access. As you click on a menu on the **Drawing** toolbar, look for a tiny gray bar at the top. Hover your mouse pointer over this bar to see the ScreenTip message, "Drag and release to make this menu float." Press and drag this bar to temporarily remove or "rip off" the menu. This process transforms the pop-out menu into a floating palette with a tiny title bar and Close box. Drag the palette around on the screen by dragging the title bar. When you are finished with the palette, click the **Close** box on the palette's title bar to put it away. The palette will merge back with the menu.

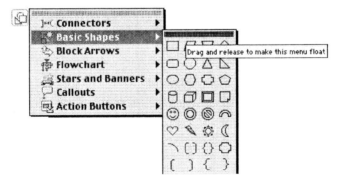

Idea: Classroom Award Certificates

Use a single slide to create an award certificate for your classroom that is easy to print and photocopy. Experiment with the lines, rectangles, and AutoShapes tools on the Drawing toolbar using this example as a guide.

Tip: The Holding Zone

The work area for slides can seem tight at times, so use the gray area around the slide as a parking spot for objects that you want to use but that are currently in the way. This area, the *pasteboard*, holds items for the current slide in use only. Items on the pasteboard won't print and won't be seen during a presentation. To see more of the pasteboard, resize the panes using the splitter bar.

 Tip: Measure Up

When working with graphic objects, it is useful to turn on the ruler. The ruler can help not only with the placement of objects on your slides, but it can also show you the size of objects created with the Drawing toolbar. To turn on the ruler, click the **View** menu and choose **Ruler**. A checkmark appears when the ruler is showing. Hide the ruler by choosing it again.

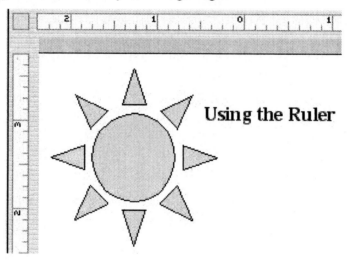

Using the Ruler

 Tip: Nudging

If you've ever wished you could move a selected object over just a little bit, then you need to learn about nudging. To nudge, select the object and then use the Drawing toolbar's **Nudge** command to move the object up, down, right, or left just a wee bit. Another way to do this is to hold down the **Command** key while pressing the up, down, right, or left arrows on the keyboard.

 Tip: Ducks in a Row

Occasionally, you may need to align objects in a row. Place your first object on the slide, format it if needed, and select it. Make another object by holding down the **Option** key and dragging to create an exact replica of the first object. Continue this process until you have the number of objects you need. Select all of the objects by clicking the first, then holding down the **Shift** key and clicking the next object in turn until all are selected. Then from the Drawing toolbar, click **Draw** and choose **Align or Distribute**. Choose the desired alignment and your objects will align themselves. Made a mistake? Press **Command-Z** to undo the alignment and then try another. To make "ducks in a row," choose **Align Top** and the top edge of the objects will be neatly aligned. Note: you can ensure they will stay aligned by grouping them. To do this, click **Draw** on the **Drawing** toolbar and choose **Group**.

Tricks: Arrays and Sweeps

An array is a series of evenly spaced (horizontal or vertical) objects, and a sweep is a series of evenly spaced objects that overlap slightly.

To create an array, select the object, click the **Edit** menu, and choose **Duplicate**. Drag the copied object to the position you want, then click the **Edit** menu and choose **Duplicate**. You can continue duplicating by pressing **Command-D** until you have all the desired objects.

Making a sweep is easy too! To make a sweep, select the object to be duplicated. Click the **Edit** menu and choose **Copy**. Then click the **Edit** menu and choose **Paste**. The copied object will slightly overlap the first object. Continue pasting until you have finished your sweep. As a shortcut, the keyboard command **Command-V** will repeat your paste command.

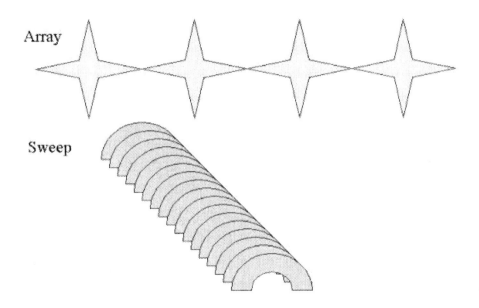

Array

Sweep

 ## Tip: The Picture Toolbar

A versatile toolbar to have at your fingertips is the Picture toolbar. This toolbar is handy for altering certain kinds of images such as the graphics in the Clip Art Gallery. It isn't usually showing so you'll have to turn it on by clicking the **View** menu and choosing **Picture** from the list of toolbars. The Picture toolbar is a floating toolbar by default so you'll need to drag it around by its title bar as needed. Experiment by inserting a graphic from the Clip Art Gallery and then use the tools such as Contrast, Brightness, and Grayscale to enhance and alter the image.

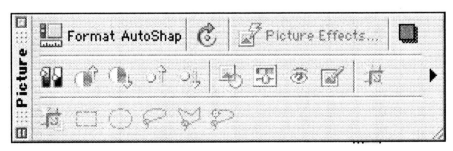

Tip: Only the Shadow Knows

Adding a shadow effect to a graphic can make a simple image seem very dramatic, especially if it is a grayscale or black and white photograph. To create a shadow, first outline your graphic or digital image with a line. To do this, first click on your graphic to select it. Then click the **Line Style** icon on the **Drawing** toolbar. Choose a line thickness suitable for your image. When you are satisfied with the effect, locate the **Shadow** icon on the **Drawing** toolbar and apply a shadow style. Use the **Shadow Setting** option to add a colored shadow.

 Trick: Export a Slide to a Graphic

If you have made a spectacular slide (or slides) and you would like to save it as a graphic to be used in other applications, you can! Be sure you have saved the slide or slides as a regular presentation first in case you decide to modify the slide later. Then click the **File** menu and choose **Save As**. Name and save your presentation as you normally do. Next, select the **File** menu and choose **Save As** again. This time, pull down the **Format** drop-down box and choose **Joint Photographic Experts Group**. Name your graphic, navigate to a saving location, and click the **Save** button. Click the Options button to have the choice of saving the current slide or more than one slide depending on what you have created. (Note: Click a checkmark in the Append file extension if you are planning to use this graphic on a Windows-based computer.)

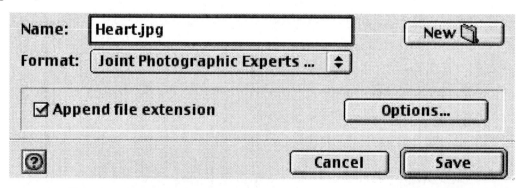

Trick: AutoShape Text and Fills

Filling an AutoShape with a picture of your own is a snap! To do this, first draw the AutoShape on your slide. (Note: Ignore the filled color because it will disappear when you fill it with your picture.) Then click on your newly drawn AutoShape to select it. On the **Drawing** toolbar, locate the **Fill** icon that looks like a paint bucket. Click on the tiny drop-down arrow next to the paint bucket and choose **Fill Effects**. The Fill Effects dialog box will open. Click the **Picture** tab. Next click the **Select Picture** button and navigate to the location where you have previously saved a graphic or picture that you wish to use. Select the graphic and the image will appear in the Picture area. This ensures that you have chosen the correct image. Now click **OK**. The AutoShape will be filled with your own graphic. (Note: you can use the same procedure to fill an AutoShape with gradients, textures, or patterns.)

Add text to your AutoShape by clicking to select the AutoShape and then just type! A text box will be created automatically. Use the tools on the Formatting toolbar or Formatting Task pane to change the font, style, color, and size.

Thinking of Printing?

 ## Trick: Don't Use the Print icon!

The Print icon on the Standard toolbar prints your slides in full size (8 ?" by 11") one after another and in full color when using a color printer. You can waste a lot of paper and color ink or toner this way! If that's what you need, fine, just click it. Otherwise, keep an open mind about printing by reading all the tips and tricks in this section.

 ## Tip: Avoid the Mud

Ink jet printers are a popular choice for home and classroom use because they are inexpensive to purchase. Think ahead! Are you planning to print out your presentation, photocopy it, and hand it out? Color printouts make for muddy or completely black graphics when reproduced by photocopying. If you'd like to conserve the color printer ink or are using a black and white laser printer, take a look at your slides before printing by using the handy **Grayscale Preview** icon on the **Standard** toolbar. This feature doesn't change your slides; it just allows them to be viewed in shades of gray. This will give you an idea of how your handouts will look.

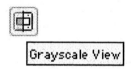

Just because you can *view* your presentation in grayscale doesn't mean it will print in grayscale. To print your color slides in grayscale you need to click the **File** menu and choose **Print**. Select the print options you desire.

 ## Tip: Accept a Handout

Examine the options for printing handouts in the Print what: section of the Print dialog box. To access this, make sure the presentation is open, then click the **File** menu and choose **Print**. Click the **Print what:** drop-down box to see that the choices are Slides, Handouts, Notes pages, and Outline view. Choose **Handouts**. The choices for handouts are 2, 3, or 6 slides per page.

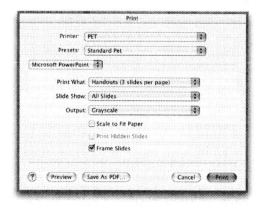

If you have a lot of small text on your slides that must be readable on your handouts, you may have to use the option of 2 or 3 slides. A favorite choice of teachers is three slides per page because it places lines for taking notes to the right of each slide.

 ## Tip: Kinds of Printouts

As you are creating your slides, you should be "scripting" what you are going to say during the presentation. Jot notes down in the **Notes** area while you create your slides. Formerly called Speaker Notes, this small area is handy for recording those brilliant things you wish to say. Later on you can access your notes by clicking the **View** menu and selecting your **Notes pages**. In this view, each slide is shown along with whatever notes you hastily jotted down. Click in the text area, adjust the view with the **Zoom** box on the **Standard** toolbar, and re-work those ideas into the witty, informative material you are going to present.

Print each one of these Notes pages to have handy as you are practicing your presentation. To do this, click the **File** menu, choose **Print**, and in the **Print What:** area, choose **Notes Pages**. The resulting printout will be an enlarged slide with your text underneath it. Note that only a certain amount of text can be added to this page.

Outlines can be printed too. For those students working in groups to develop a presentation, it is useful for each student to have a copy of the outline to help them develop their speech. This is a good alternative to having a printout of each slide, and it will save classroom toner/ink and paper. To print in outline form, click the **File** menu, choose **Print**, and in the **Print What:** area, choose **Outline View**.

Idea: Overhead Transparencies

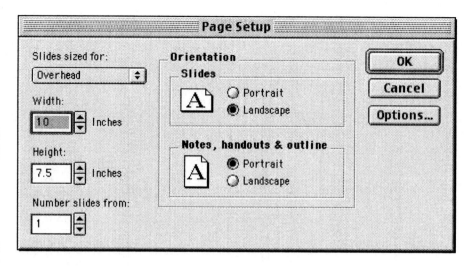

Many classrooms and schools have a single projection device which must be shared among all the teachers. If you have created a *PowerPoint* presentation and the projection device is not available, consider purchasing some ink jet or laser printer overhead transparency film. You can print each slide on a transparency and use them on the more readily available overhead projector. To print on transparencies, click the **File** menu and choose **Page Setup**. Click the **Slides sized for:** drop-down box and choose **Overhead**. Then print the currently selected slide by clicking the **File** menu, choosing **Print**, and in the **Print Range** section, choosing **Current Slide**. (By the way, be sure you are using the correct transparency film for your printer. Laser transparency film is special in that it will not melt with the heat of laser printing. Ink jet film is right for printing with color ink.)

 ## Tip: Make a Storyboard

To allow students to draft their own presentations, create a "blank slide" presentation with three empty slides. Print it as a three-slide handout with lines to use as a graphic organizer or storyboard. Students can sketch out their slides in the blank slide areas, and jot down notes for each slide on this storyboard.

Trick: Send it to Word

For more control over your printouts, *PowerPoint* presentations can be sent to Word where you can add your own touches. (Note that this doesn't change your slides in any way.) In Word, you can add headers and footers such as your name, the date, school name, and page numbers. This feature is most useful for writing up your full presentation for a stress-free delivery day or an emergency fill-in presenter. A final reason to bring your slides into a Word document is to share a presentation with a fellow colleague or student who doesn't have *PowerPoint* but has Word.

Fast Learning for Teachers

 ## Tip: Visit Mactopia

Visit Microsoft's official Web site for Macintosh enthusiasts (http://www.microsoft.com/mac) to read articles, tips, and hints for *PowerPoint* users of all levels of experience. If you are thinking of upgrading to a newer version of Office for the Macintosh, this is a free way to preview new features. There's also a support area where you can look up answers to the mysteries of why *PowerPoint* does (or doesn't do) what you want.

 ## Tip: Useful Keyboard Shortcuts

It's not hard to find useful keyboard shortcuts for *PowerPoint*. Conduct a search for "**keyboard shortcuts**" in *PowerPoint* Help. Many keyboard shortcuts you have learned for Microsoft Word will work too, especially with text in placeholders. For those cross-platform users of *PowerPoint* for Windows and Macintosh be aware that not all keyboard shortcuts work the same way in both platforms.

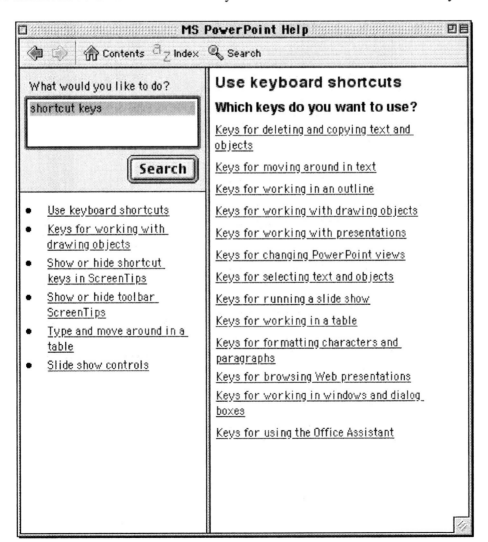

Jazzing it Up!

Before venturing into the wonderful world of multimedia, it is wise to pause and think about providing your audience or classroom with solid content, well-designed slides, and a powerfully-built plan of delivery. When working with students on presentations, mentoring students in these areas is essential. When it comes to adding "bells and whistles," students will swiftly grasp using transitions, animations, sounds, and movies. Each new version of *PowerPoint* adds yet more special effects, so there's always more to learn.

 ## Tip: Resist Transition Temptation (OS X refer to page 38)

Transitions are effects that occur as you move from one slide to the next slide. Transitions should be used to visually guide your audience's attention from one slide to another. Pick one transition to use with all of the slides in your presentation. Avoid headaches; decide on a transition and use it consistently in each presentation.

 ## Tip: Just Passing Through

Transitions are best applied using the Slide Sorter view. When a transition is applied to a slide, a transition icon appears below it. This visual helps you easily identify which slides have transitions and which don't. To apply the same transition to all slides, click the **Edit** menu and choose **Select All**. (Note: the selected slides will have a heavy outline box around them.) *PowerPoint* 2001 users will see the **Slide Sorter** toolbar appear. Select a transition from the drop-down list. After applying a transition(s), click on the icon that appears below the slide to "play" the transition so you can see how it works in your presentation.

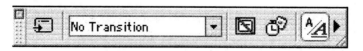

The speed of how a transition plays can be important. Applied transitions are supposed to catch the audience's attention without mesmerizing them. To adjust the speed of a transition, *PowerPoint* 2001 users can open the **Slide Transition** dialog box from the **Slide Sorter** toolbar or click the **Slide Show** menu, and then choose **Slide Transition**. The Formatting palette can also be used to apply or change a transition. Remember, slow, medium, or fast speeds are quite subjective as computers vary in power. A more powerful computer will allow for faster transitions. Think of slower computers or slides heavy in graphics as speed bumps.

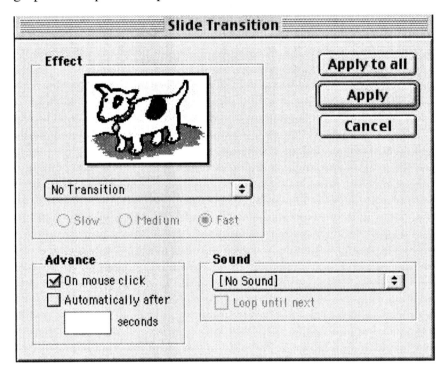

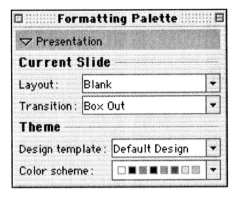

 ## Trick: Dysfunctional Transitions

Have students create a four-slide presentation on a topic they know well. Assign each student a transition or two to use consistently in their mini-presentation. Ask each student to write a description of the transition's action (the transition name can help in this). Ask students if the speed improves or detracts from the transition. Make a classroom list of the purposes and critiques of the transitions.

 ## Trick: Teachers in Control

Build "effective use of multimedia" into the rubrics used to assess student presentations. Also, because of limited classroom time for presenting slide shows, decide how many transitions and animations students will use *before* they create their slides.

Tip: EZ Animation

Use Animations to do quick animations of graphic objects and text placeholders on your slides. *PowerPoint* animation is the term used to describe how an object or a group of text appears on a slide. Some of these "pre-packaged" groups of effects are for graphics and some are for text. Depending on what you have selected - text or graphic - the available animations will be displayed.

PowerPoint 2001 users can apply a preset animation scheme in Normal or Slide Sorter View. For Normal view, click the text or select the graphic object you wish to animate. Click the **Slide Show** menu and choose **Animations**. The animations appear in the sub-menu. Be sure to notice that the first choice is OFF. If you decide to remove an animation, you will need to return here to turn it off. In Slide Sorter View, apply a preset animation from the **Slide Sorter** toolbar. To preview an animation, click the **Slide Show** menu and choose **Animation Preview**. For power users, there is a handy Animation toolbar. Use it by first clicking the **View** menu, then choosing **Toolbars** and finally, selecting **Animation Effects Toolbar**.

Use the **Formatting** toolbar to change animation effects quickly. There is also an effect called No Animation that can be used to remove an applied animation.

After applying text/object animations to your slides, be sure to run your presentation to see the full effect. If you applied your effects in Normal view, running the presentation is the only way to see the animation(s). In **Slide Sorter** view, click the small icon under each slide to play the animation. Always run the entire show to view the complete effect of the animations.

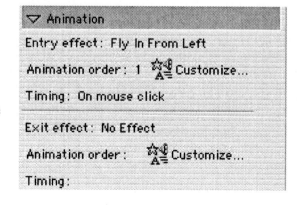

Tip: Building Text Animations

Somehow, dancing alphabets come to mind when thinking of animated text! Early versions of *PowerPoint* called the process of animating text "building the text," and it has long been a staple of business users of *PowerPoint*. Designed to be suspenseful, they are called builds because of their "one after another" appearance on the screen to build on previous comments or ideas. Preset or Animation schemes applied to text are for title and body placeholders only. Text is then treated as a group and is animated paragraph by paragraph (which may be bullet by bullet). The only way to animate text word-by-word or letter-by-letter is to create a Custom Animation.

Before applying these text animations consider what you will be saying while the text appears on the screen. If you are handing out your presentation in printed form to your class or audience prior to the presentation, most participants will have read what you were hoping would be suspenseful before they see it, thus ruining the effect. Also, it takes longer to present material one line at a time. Try one of the text animations on the first slide in your presentation to learn how to use them. Animations can be applied to text on one slide using Normal View or to one or all slides in Slide Sorter View.

 ## Trick: Use Animated GIFs

PowerPoint 2001 was the first version of *PowerPoint* for Macintosh to allow the use of animated GIFs. These graphics are pre-created in a special application and animate on their own without applying any animations from *PowerPoint*. Many are available for free on the Internet and there are some in the Clip Art Gallery. Note that animated GIFs won't "*move*" until you run the presentation.

 ## Tip: Effects of Custom Animation

If you'd like to exert more control over the animations you are using, then working with the Custom Animations of *PowerPoint* is right for you. It can take a lot of time to explore these special techniques so only a few will be covered here.

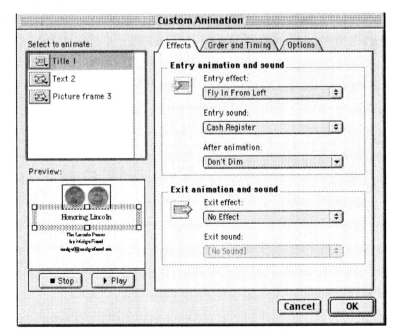

Many teachers enjoy the visual effects of the animations but dislike the screeching brakes, whooshing, and breaking glass sounds of which students are so fond. These sound effects can be silenced. If multiple animations have been applied to one slide, use the Custom Animation controls to decide which plays first. The best way to learn Customized Animations is to experiment with the options and decide which are best for you.

PowerPoint 2001 users can access the Custom Animation controls by selecting a slide to work with in **Normal** view, clicking the **Slide Show** menu, choosing **Animations**, and then selecting **Custom**. The tabs in the Custom Animation dialog box allow you to manipulate the objects on this *currently selected* slide. In this tip, the Effects tab will be explored.

Use the settings under the **Effects** tab to decide which object(s) to animate with which effect. First, select the object in the **Select to animate** section in the upper left-hand corner by clicking a checkmark next to the name of the object. Use the Preview box to the right to see that you have chosen the correct object.

In the **Entry animation and sound** section, first choose an animation effect from the drop-down box. When you choose one, its direction of entry will appear. If you wish to use an entry sound, choose that from the **Entry sound** drop-down box. In the **Exit animation and sound** section, choose what you would like to have happen when the animation(s) is finished. This is much like a transition.

If the object is text, click the **Options** tab. In the **Select to animate** section in the upper left-hand corner, click the drop-down arrow to activate a text entry, text exit, or both. When activated, that section of the Options tab will be available and you can select the text animation options. Click **OK** when you have finished with your custom animation for one, several, or all of the selected objects.

Presentable Presentations

 ## Tip: Presentation Types

Most of the time, *PowerPoint* presentations are designed to be "instructor-led." Teachers find *PowerPoint* presentations are effective for sharing information with students in a direct manner. In addition, student projects created and presented by a team of students is an equally effective "instructor-led" model. But, there is another type of presentation that teachers and students can use: a "self-running" or kiosk presentation. Educators find many uses for this design, from tutorials for students who were absent, to open house presentations, to retirement and party-related shows.

 ## Tip: Hands-Free Presentations

To set up a kiosk presentation, first click the **Slide Show** menu and then choose **Set Up Show**. The Set Up Show dialog box appears. In the **Show type** section, click to select **Browsed at a kiosk**. This will set the screen show to fit the entire monitor screen. In the **Advance slides** section click to select the **Using timings, if present**. Click **OK** to exit this dialog box.

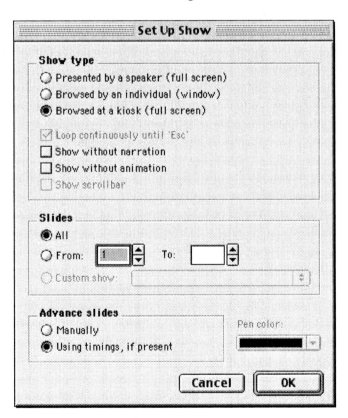

Power Point 2001 users can set the timings of the slides with the Slide Transition dialog box. Click the **Slide Show** menu and choose **Slide Transitions**. In the **Advance** section, uncheck the **On Mouse Click** and click in the **Automatically after** box. Set the time in this box to the number of seconds you think is appropriate for your audience or classroom, and then click **Apply to All**. If the show plays too fast or too slow, you can always return to this dialog box and adjust this setting.

Trick: Concerned About Time?

If you are concerned about the amount of time that your students need to view slides in a presentation that runs automatically, then teach them to control the advancement of slides by clicking the mouse. In the **Slide Transition** dialog box or the **Slide Transition** task pane's **Advance Slide** area, make sure **On Mouse Click** is selected.

 ## Tip: Rehearse Timings

To accurately set timings for slide shows that advance automatically, click the **Slide Show** menu and choose **Rehearse Timings**. A special timer section will appear in the lower right-hand corner that shows the elapsed time. When you think enough time has passed, press the **Spacebar** or the **Page Down** key to move to the next slide. When you reach the end, you will be asked if you want to keep the slide timings for this show. Choose **Yes** to keep the timings.

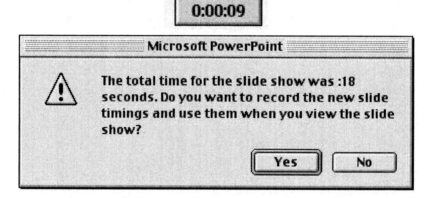

 ## Trick: Double-Click Slide Shows (OS X users refer to page 40)

If you would like your students to run slide shows without having to locate and launch *PowerPoint*, and without having to deal with the *PowerPoint* interface, try saving your *PowerPoint* presentation in a special "show" format. First, just to be safe, save your presentation as you normally do. Then, click the **File** menu and choose **Save As**. In the **Save as Type** drop-down box, choose *PowerPoint* **Show (*pps)**. Give this file a name that is different from your regular *PowerPoint* presentation so you'll be able to tell them apart. Click **Save**. Now your students can simply select this file to automatically run the show. Don't forget to select **Append file extension** if you plan to show this presentation on a Windows-based computer.

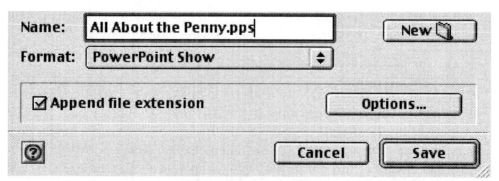

Special Project: Play Audio CD Tracks in a Presentation

Step One: Decide on a CD track to use

Check to be sure that you have working speakers on the computer(s) you will be using to create and present the presentation. Audio CDs will play on your computer in multiple applications. AppleCD Audio Player and iTunes are two of the most popular applications. Place the audio CD in the CD drive and play the track you wish to use, noting the song track number and the start and end track timings.

Step Two: Insert the Audio CD

Exit the application that played the CD. You will have to do this each time you run this presentation. Remember, once you insert an audio track to play in a presentation, you must have the CD in the CD drive each time you run the presentation.

Step Three: Insert the CD icon into the presentation

Move to the slide where you wish to play the audio track. Click the **Insert** menu and choose **Movies and Sound**, and then select **Play CD Audio Track**. *PowerPoint* 2001 users will see the **Play Options** dialog box appear.

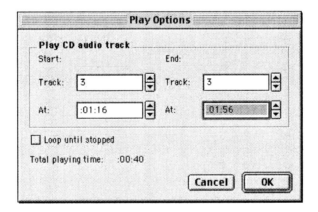

In the section **Play CD audio track**, enter the starting track number and ending track number. If you are playing just a portion of the track, enter the exact track time in the start and end boxes. The total playing time will appear for your settings. If you want the track to play over and over, select the **Loop until stopped** box. After you click **OK**, a message will appear asking if you wish the sound to play automatically or if you wish to start the track by clicking on the CD sound icon.

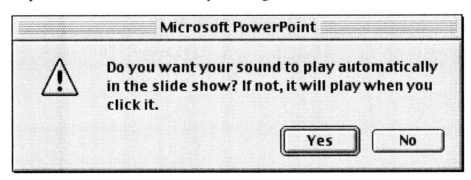

Step Four: The CD Icon

The CD icon will appear on your slide. This is an object that can be moved and resized. Move it to a spot on the slide away from other objects. If you are planning to click on it to play the audio CD track, then it is advisable to make it larger so it can be easily seen.

Step Five: Customize the Sound

From the **Slide Show** menu, choose **Animations** and then **Custom**. *PowerPoint* 2001 users will see the **Custom Animation** dialog box appear. Notice the option to **Hide while not playing**. If the sound is set to automatically play then select this option. If you need to adjust which track plays, click the **CD Options** button to open the **Sound Options** dialog box. Click **OK** when you are finished.

Step Six: Play the CD Audio Track

Test your presentation with your audio file set. If possible, go to the computer where you will be presenting this audio linked presentation to make sure it plays as you intended. *Don't forget, you need to have the audio CD with you!*

Beyond the blue horizon
Waits a beautiful day.
Goodbye to things that bore me.
Joy is waiting for me.
I see a new horizon.
My life has only begun.
Beyond the blue horizon
Lies a rising sun.

*Leo Robin, Richard A. Whiting and W. Franke Harling

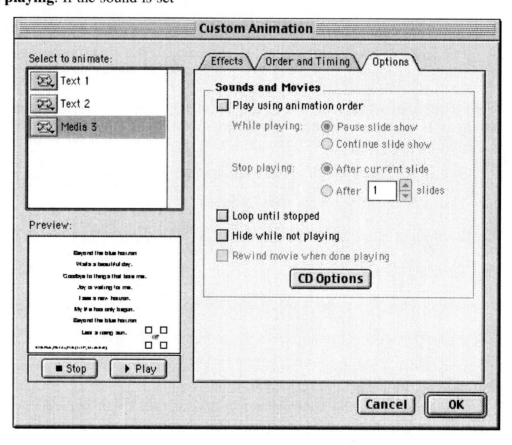

Step Seven: Other Audio Options

Audio files can be very large in file size. If you have audio files stored on your hard drive, you can play them as sound files. (Note: this is a different procedure than previously given for the Audio CD Track.) To begin, click the **Insert** menu, choose **Movies and Sounds**, and choose **Sound from File**. Navigate to the location on your hard drive where your audio clip is stored and insert it. This sound will be embedded into your presentation, and will increase the file size. Note that not all sound files can be used, especially very large files.

Special Project: Create PowerPoint Movies

This special feature of *PowerPoint* 2001 and *PowerPoint* X allows you to create easy-to-view movies in a special QuickTime movie format. This is useful for showing a presentation to a user who doesn't have *PowerPoint* but who can download and install QuickTime. QuickTime Player is a free application for both the Windows and Macintosh platforms.

These *PowerPoint* movies offer you a great way to share your dazzling digital images as a photo album movie. First create a presentation with your digital images and captions, and then save it as you would any other presentation. Then, follow these steps to create a *PowerPoint* movie:

Step One: Plan Ahead!

PowerPoint presentations that will become *PowerPoint* movies must be designed and developed differently. Avoid adding custom animation features, action buttons, and hyperlinks to Web pages or other presentations. These special effects features may not work in a presentation saved as a *PowerPoint* movie. If you are planning to create movies that will be shown on the Windows platform, be sure to save your pictures in GIF or JPG format, and use fonts that are common to both Macintosh and Windows computers. If you use the special QuickTime transitions, be sure to test the movie on a Windows computer before presenting it.

Step Two: Add Slide Timings

Select all of your slides by switching to **Slide Sorter** view, clicking the **Edit** menu, and choosing **Select All**. Alternatively, press **Command-A** on the keyboard. Next, click the **Slide Show** menu and choose **Slide Transition**. Select the **Automatically after** checkbox and enter a desired number of seconds. (Note: Enter at least 5 seconds. If you have slides with a lot of text, enter more than 5 seconds.) Click the **Apply to All** button to apply this timing to all of the slides.

Step Three: Save Your Presentation

Be sure to save your *PowerPoint* presentation as you normally do before transforming it into a *PowerPoint* movie. By doing this, you can always return to your original creation if the resulting movie isn't exactly to your liking. You can edit *PowerPoint* movies, but you may wish to use the presentation in a non-movie format at some other time.

Step Four: Make a Movie

Learn the movie-creation process by first using a pre-existing presentation containing simple text and graphic layouts. To create a movie, click the **File** menu and choose **Make Movie**. The **Save** dialog box opens. (Note: Select **Append file extension** if you are planning to show your movie on a Windows computer.)

Choose a saving location. Name the movie something different than the presentation so that you can easily distinguish between the two. Then, click the **Adjust settings** button and then the **Next** button. The **Movie Options** dialog box will open. In this dialog box you will select certain features for your movie.

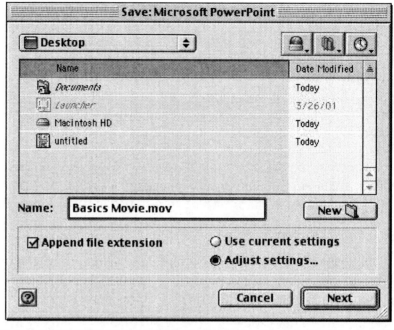

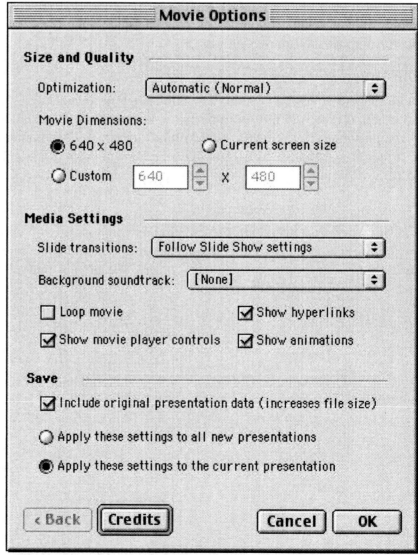

First, in the **Size and Quality** section, use the **Optimization** drop-down box to choose a quality for the resulting movie. For most productions, **Automatic (Normal)** will be fine. If you desire a higher-quality movie, you can select your preferences here in the areas of size, smooth playback, and quality. Next, use the **Movie Dimensions** box to set the size of your movie. For most movies, 640 x 480 is the right choice, but you may wish to use a custom setting of anywhere from 100 x 100 to 2000 x 2000. Most monitors can play movies smoothly at 800 x 600 and 1024 x 768.

Second, examine the section called **Media Settings**. If you created a presentation with slide transitions already applied, select **Follow Slide Show Settings**. Alternatively, you can add a special QuickTime transition with this drop-down box. QuickTime transitions have been created especially for use with this movie format. QuickTime transitions look wonderful in movies played only on a Macintosh.

If you wish to add a background soundtrack, add it here rather than during the presentation-creation process. It will play more smoothly when added here. (Note: the audio CD must be in the CD drive to play a background track.) Always check the **Show movie player controls** so that viewers have control when playing your *PowerPoint* movie. Also, if you used hyperlinks and animations in your previously created presentation, check those areas in this section. (Remember that not all animations and hyperlinks work in *PowerPoint* movies as they are intended. Check Microsoft's Mactopia Web site regularly for more information.) For a self-running presentation, click **Loop Movie**.

Lastly, explore the options in the **Save** section. If you want to edit the resulting *PowerPoint* movie, be sure to select **Include original presentation data**. This will result in a larger file size, but it may be worth it. Decide whether these settings are to be used with just this one presentation or if you would like to keep these settings for all the movies you create in the future. You may decide to add your name, a copyright date, and a summary by clicking the **Credits** button.

When you have set all of your options, click the **OK** button to return to the **Save** dialog box, and click **OK** again to save your movie.

If you find that you need to adjust the Movie Options settings in a saved movie, launch *PowerPoint* and open the movie by clicking the **File** menu and choosing **Open**. Once your movie is open, select the **File** menu and choose **Make Movie** again. Use the **Adjust** menu button to access the **Movie Options** dialog box. Make your changes and re-save the movie.

Step Five: Double-click the movie

Double-click your *PowerPoint* movie. QuickTime Player will automatically launch and then play the movie. Use the QuickTime movie controls and menu choices to control your movie.

Special Note: Know your (Teacher) Preferences

If your students are creating *PowerPoint* movies and you don't want them to adjust the settings in the Movie Options dialog box, set your preferences by following these steps. First click the **Edit** menu and choose **Preferences**. On the **General** tab, click the **Movie Options** button to open the **Movie Options** dialog box. Select your preferred settings and in the **Save** area, click the **Apply these settings to all presentations**. Click **OK**, and then click **OK** again in the **Preferences** dialog box. When students create movies, simply choose **Use current settings** in the **Save** dialog box instead of the Adjust settings button. These preferences will be used for all the future movie presentations that are created.

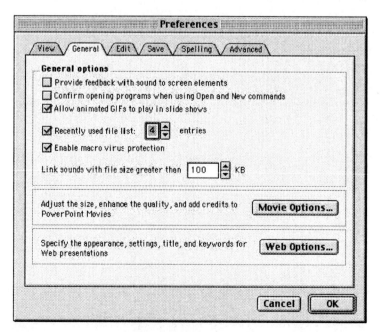

Microsoft PowerPoint X

Microsoft PowerPoint X, was created for use with the OS X operating system. It looks a little different due to the look of the Aqua interface, but many of the same menus and options still exist.

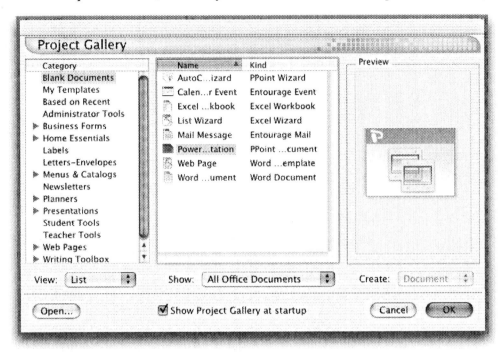

The Preferences menu, which appeared before in the Tools menu, can now be found in the **PowerPoint** menu. This is where you can set your personal options, including your viewing, editing, and spelling preferences.

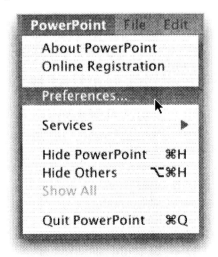

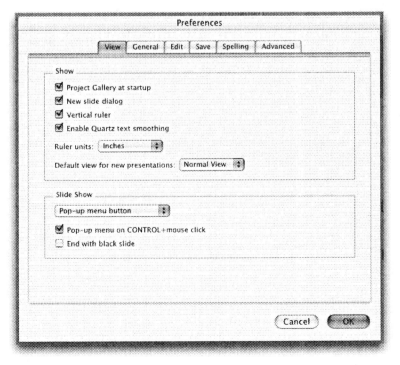

PowerPoint X *(cont.)*

PowerPoint X gives you even more transition options for your presentations. You now have the option of using *QuickTime* transitions for an enhanced multimedia experience.

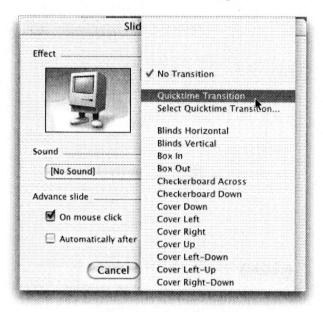

Transition options include cross Fade, Explode, Implode, and Zoom. When you click on each option, you can personalize your presentation even further by selecting colors, percentages of transparency, areas on the screen where you want the transition to start, and more.

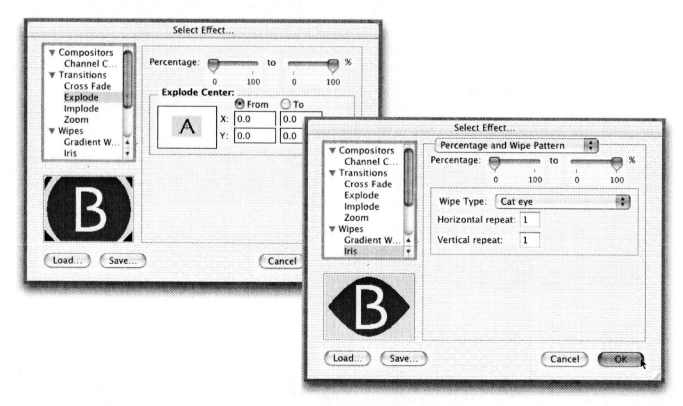

PowerPoint X *(cont.)*

You have more control over the graphics in your presentation with the option to set the percentage of transparency for your graphics. For example, if you have a graphic like a school logo or a photo that you are using as a background image on a slide, you can select the exact degree of transparency that you want it to have. The results can make your presentation even more visually stunning! You can find this option on the Formatting Palette under **Fill and Line**, which appears when you click on a graphic.

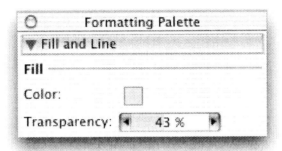

You can also click on the graphic and select **Format—Picture**. The Transparency option is found on the **Colors and Lines** tab.

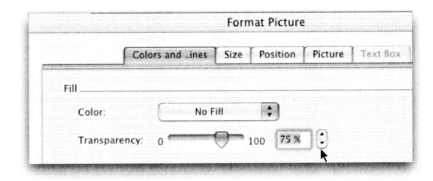

Graphic at 0%transparency

Graphic at 65% transparency

PowerPoint X *(cont.)*

With *PowerPoint X*, you have the option of saving your presentation as a *PowerPoint* package. This allows you to save your presentation and any supporting files in one place. Your supporting files might be other documents that you link to, or sound and movies that you include. Everything is saved in the same folder, which you can immediately transfer to another computer or burn onto a CD.

To use this feature, go to the **File** menu and select **Save As...**. Under **Format:**, select **PowerPoint Package**.

With OS X, you also have the option of creating a PDF file of your presentation. To do this, go to the **File** menu and select **Print**. Select the **Save as PDF** button. Decide where you want to save your PDF and click the **Save** button.

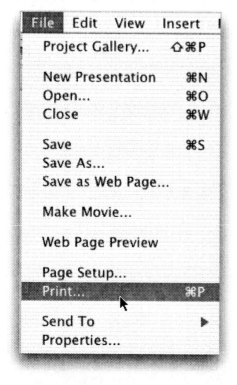

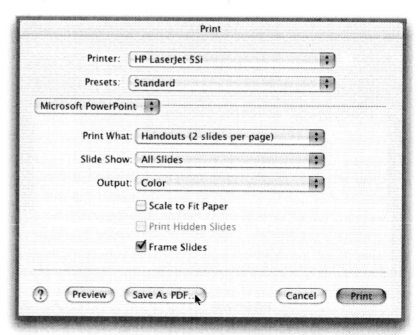

Editor
Amy Gammill, M. Ed.

Editorial Project Manager
Elizabeth Morris, Ph.D.

Editor-in-Chief
Sharon Coan, M.S. Ed.

Cover Artist
Lesley Palmer

Art Coordinator
Kevin Barnes

Art Director
CJae Froshay

Imaging
Alfred Lau

Product Manager
Phil Garcia

Acknowledgements
Microsoft Office© is 1991-2003
Microsoft Corporation. All rights
reserved. *Microsoft PowerPoint* is a
trademark of Microsoft Corporation,
registered in the U.S. and other
countries.

Publishers
Rachelle Cracchiolo, M.S. Ed.
Mary Dupuy Smith, M.S. Ed.

Author

Midge Frazel

Teacher Created Materials, Inc.
6421 Industry Way
Westminster, CA 92683
www.teachercreated.com
ISBN-0-7439-3816-X
©2003 Teacher Created Materials, Inc.
Reprinted, 2004
Made in U.S.A.

Table of Contents

Introduction

If you've taken a basic workshop—or explored *Microsoft PowerPoint* on your own—and can now construct a simple presentation, then it is time to make your presentations and slide shows into something really special. Step up to another level by learning some simple tricks that will make your presentations look professionally created. At the same time gather some tips to make it all a little easier.

The tips and tricks in this book are aimed at educators who are preparing to use *PowerPoint* as a teaching tool or as a productivity tool for their students. No matter what your subject or grade level, use *PowerPoint* to improve the delivery of your curriculum content. In addition, by using *PowerPoint* you can motivate and model the use of technology in the classroom. Whether you are using *PowerPoint* to present information to students for note-taking, or as a one-computer tutorial for delivery of content to enhance student instruction, this book offers ideas and shortcuts to save time in preparing and delivering instructional material.

Today's students are motivated to learn in different ways than previous generations of learners. As a multimedia instruction tool, *PowerPoint* can help teachers cover material quickly and easily in a medium suited to this technologically-oriented generation.

If you are a teacher who uses PowerPoint on both Windows and Macintosh computers, this book is an excellent cross-platform resource. It has been divided into two sections, one for Windows users and the other for Macintosh users of PowerPoint. The Windows section has been prepared for presentations created with PowerPoint 2000 (part of Office 2000) and PowerPoint 2002 (part of Office XP). These instructions can be found on pages 4--39 of this side of the book.

If you flip the book over, you will find the Macintosh instructions for *Tips and Tricks for Using Microsoft PowerPoint.* The Macintosh section has been prepared for presentations created with *PowerPoint* 2001 (part of Office 2001). If you are using Office: mac v x on your computer, the same instructions will apply. The interface will appear on your screen looking just a bit differently than the screenshots in this book. If you have an earlier version of *PowerPoint*, many of these tips and tricks will still work for you.

The author of this book has a resource page for *PowerPoint* users located at
http://www.midgefrazel.net/powerpoint.html
It is filled with links to current Web resources such as tutorials and multimedia resources appropriate for classroom use.

So, power on your computer, start *PowerPoint*, and start reading.

Slide Creation Time Savers

Slide Layouts

Planning and developing each slide in a presentation takes the largest amount of time. Writing and editing the content and planning the delivery are the bulk of the work of presentation design. In this section you will find some timesaving ideas for basic slide creation.

 **Tip: Detour Ahead!**

Create your title slide first, and then decide on one of the slide layouts for the majority of the rest of your slides. Create several slides with that layout before you add content. You can always change the slide layout later or even delete unneeded slides. Having the slides ready will make adding and editing your content faster.

To quickly create a new slide with the same layout as the one chosen previously, follow the appropriate instructions below:

PowerPoint 2000 users can hold down the **Shift** key on the keyboard while clicking the **New Slide** icon on the **Standard** toolbar.

PowerPoint 2002 users can simply click the **New Slide** icon on the **Formatting** toolbar to have the **Slide Layout** task pane pop into view. The task pane makes choosing the same or different slide layouts an easy click and is new to *PowerPoint* 2002. The slide layout currently chosen will be selected if the **Show when inserting new slides message** is checked.

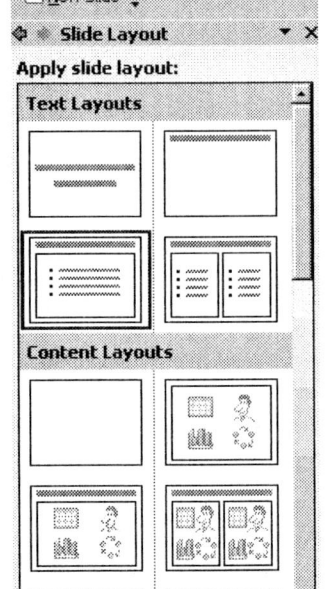

 **Tip: Selecting is Imperative**

It can't be emphasized enough that items placed on *PowerPoint* slides must be selected in order to make changes to them. Most of the time, you can tell if something is selected by the appearance of selection handles. If you are struggling to manipulate something on a slide, check to see if the object is selected. If not, click on the object to select it and try again.

Selection handle

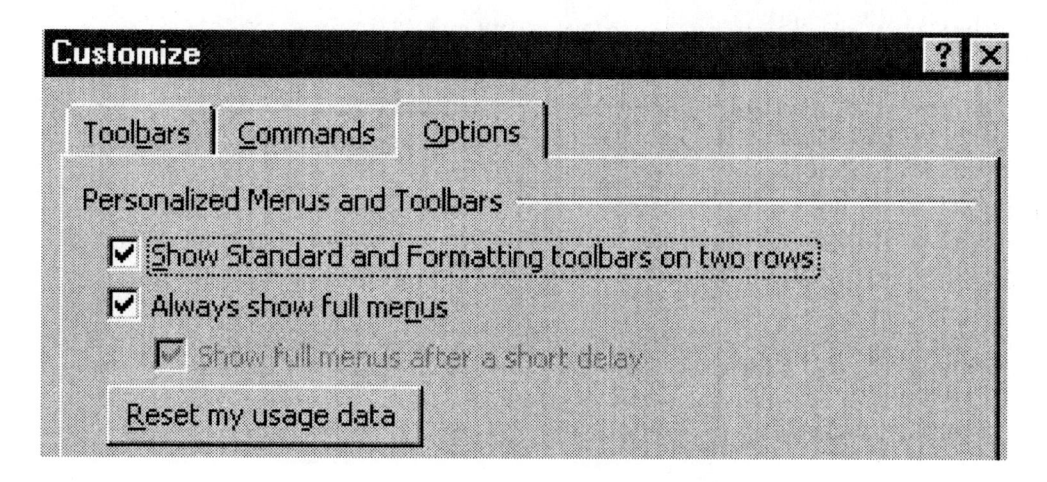

Tip: Separate Toolbars

To allow for more room on the screen, the Standard and Formatting toolbars share one row. If you'd like to see the icons on the Formatting toolbar more clearly, click the **Tools** menu and choose **Customize**. Click the **Options** tab and select **Show Standard and Formatting toolbars on two rows**.

Tip: Adjusting the Panes

If you like creating your slides in Normal view so that you can work on the current slide, the outline, and notes all at once, then learn to adjust the size of these panes to increase or decrease each one as needed. Place your cursor over the heavy line (called the splitter bar) located between panes. The cursor should transform into a two-headed arrow. When you see this arrow, simply click and hold, then drag to resize the pane.

Trick: Putting Panes Back to Normal

If you are sharing a computer with others or are responsible for a group of computers in a classroom, library, or lab setting, it is inevitable that users will resize the panes and create a maintenance headache.

Users of *PowerPoint 2000* can resize the panes to the default setting by pressing the **Shift** key and clicking the **Normal View** button. Sadly, this handy trick is not available in *PowerPoint* 2002.

 ## Tip: Change the Bullets

The Slide AutoLayouts that contain bulleted text allow for quick entry of important text and phrases. Jazz them up by changing the way the bullets appear on your slide. First, on a bulleted slide, click within the typed bulleted text. From the **Format** menu, choose **Bullets and Numbering**. In the **Bullets and Numbering** dialog box, click the **Bulleted** tab. Examine the available styles, click on one to choose it, and then click **OK**.

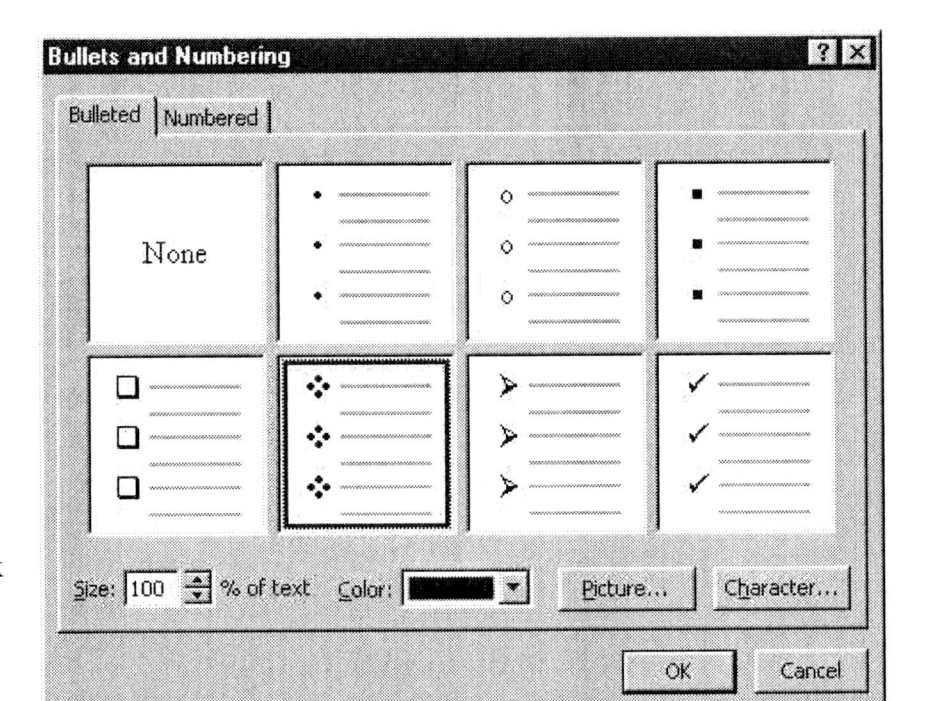

 ## Trick: Tricky Bullets

If the sample styles for the bulleted text aren't fancy enough, you can change them to tiny "pictures" instead. Customized bullets (often called characters) are made from special symbols in a font. In the **Bullets and Numbering** dialog box with the **Bulleted** tab selected, click on the button labeled **Customize or Character**. In the next dialog box, use the **Font** drop down list to choose an installed font.

You can also use your own graphic as a bullet. Of course the graphic must be very small in size and stored on your hard drive. If you have one you'd like to use, click the **Picture** button to open the **Picture Bullet** dialog box in the **Clip Organizer**. Click the **Import Clips** or **Import** button to locate your graphic.

Tip: Duplicate Your Favorite Slide

You might be tempted to copy and paste objects from one slide to another but it is easier to duplicate an entire slide and then eliminate or edit the objects on it. Why work so hard? To do this, select the slide, click the **Insert** menu and choose **Duplicate Slide**. An exact copy of the entire slide will be inserted.

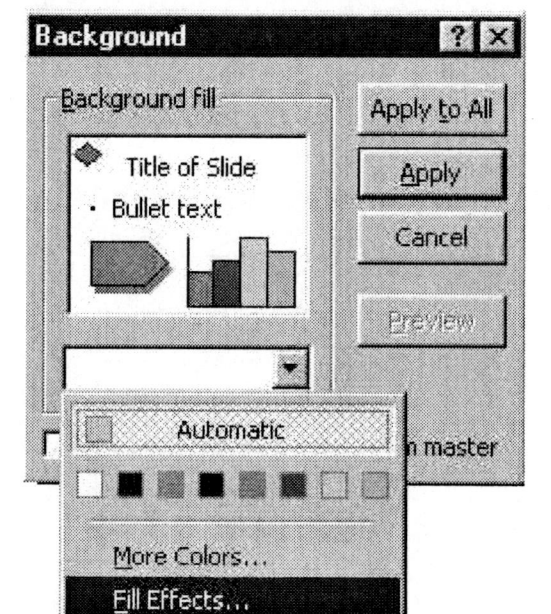

Trick: Picture Backgrounds

Your students will enjoy using digital photographs for their reports. To use a digital image as a background for the slides, click the **Format** menu and choose **Background**. Click the **Background Fill** drop-down list and choose **Fill Effects**. Select the **Picture** tab.

Next click the **Select Picture** button and navigate to the location where your images are stored. Select the image you desire and it will appear (along with its filename), as will a sample of how it will look on your slide. Click **OK** to choose the image. The **Background** dialog box appears again to confirm your choice. Click the **Apply** button to add the image to the slide.

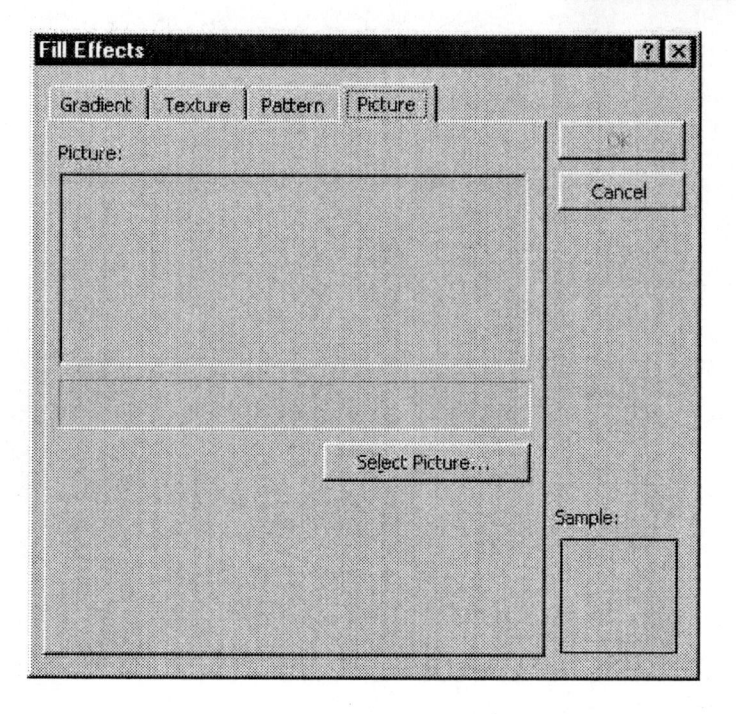

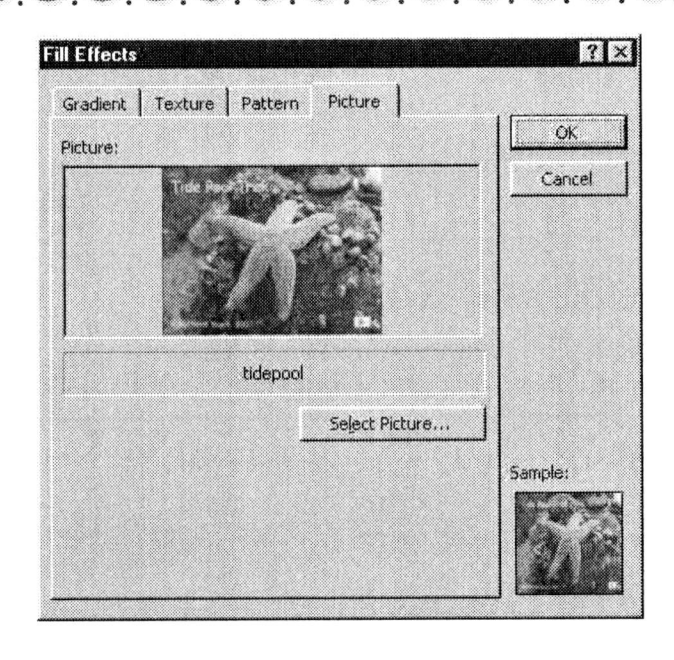

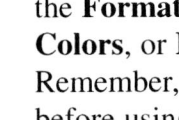 ## Tip: Background Check

You can also fill the background of your slides with a solid color, shaded gradient, or a texture. Click the **Format** menu and choose **Background**. In the **Background** dialog box, choose a color, **More Colors**, or **Fill Effects**. When using Fill Effects, experiment with the choices in each tabbed section. Remember, your background, text colors, and graphics have to work nicely together so think carefully before using an orange plaid texture as a filled background!

 ## Idea: Digital Image Title Slides

Digital images from your school field trips make excellent title slides for multimedia reports that summarize class experiences. Since text is hard to read on highly colored backgrounds, change the text to a complementary light color for easy readability. (Photograph taken by Kathleen Wasik, fourth grade teacher, Hull, Massachusetts.)

 **Trick: Blank is Good**

After designing your title slide, try creating the rest of your slides with the blank (white) background. As you place images or drawn objects on your slides, you may discover that a highly colored background will detract from your message and may make your text unreadable from a distance. Concentrate on the purpose of your presentation. You can always add a background or a design template to your slides after you have created them.

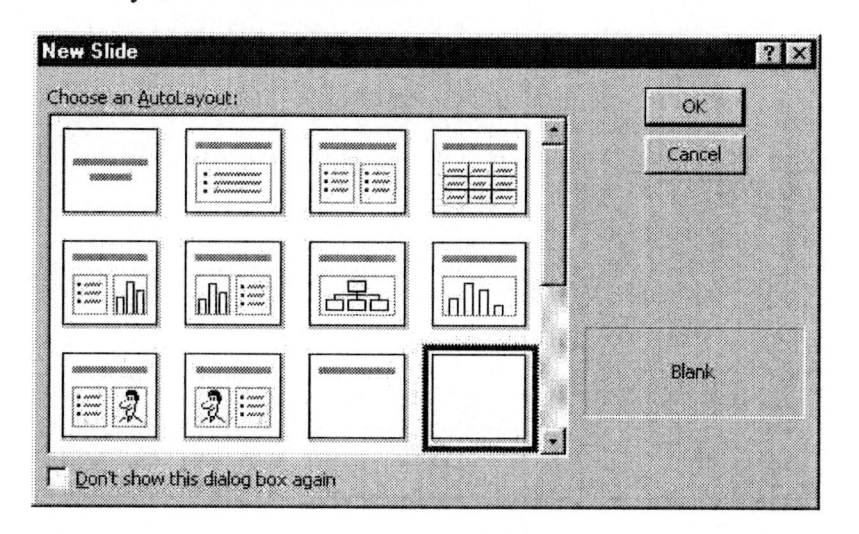

Tip: Selecting Slides in Slide Sorter View

Experienced *PowerPoint* users know that the easiest way to view and select multiple slides is by using the Slide Sorter view. To select multiple slides, first click the **View** menu and choose **Slide Sorter** or click the **Slide Sorter View** icon in the **Views** area. Then click the **Edit** menu and choose **Select All**. Remember, slides that have been selected have a heavy border around them in **Slide Sorter View**. To deselect slides, simply click in the white area between slides.

Often you may need to select just a group of slides. Select consecutive or adjacent slides by holding down the **Shift** key while clicking the beginning and ending slide. All the slides between them will be selected. To select non-adjacent slides hold down the **Ctrl** key and click each slide. Below, non-consecutive slides (2, 4, 9, and 12) have been selected.

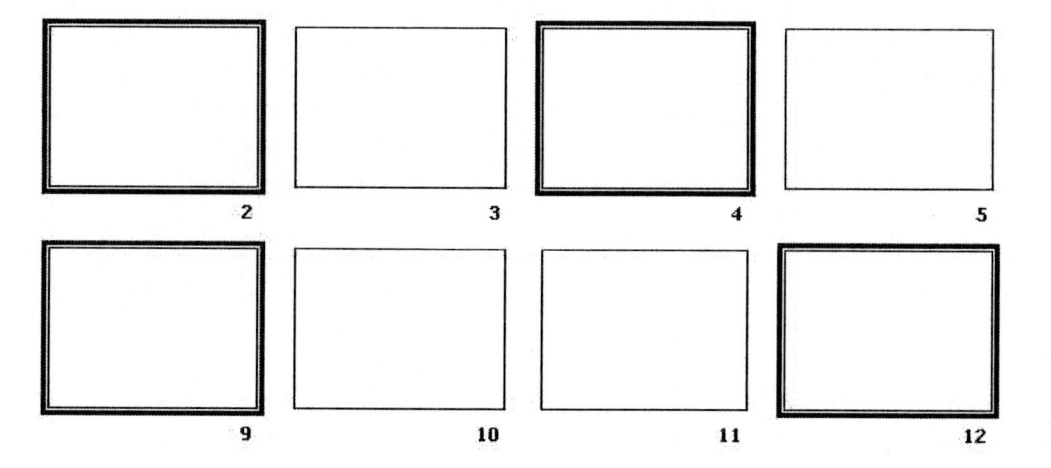

 **Tip: Sum It Up**

Want to make sure your students get the main points of the lesson you presented using *PowerPoint*? First, be sure the main points are typed in the title text AutoLayout placeholder on each slide. Then switch to **Slide Sorter** view. Select the slides, then click the **Summary Slide** icon on the **Slide Sorter** toolbar. This will create a slide with all of the title text of the slides you selected. This slide will be placed in front of the first slide you selected but since you are in Slide Sorter view, you can move this slide to the end (or wherever you desire). Don't forget to change the title text on this new slide from "Summary Slide" to something more appropriate for your lesson summary.

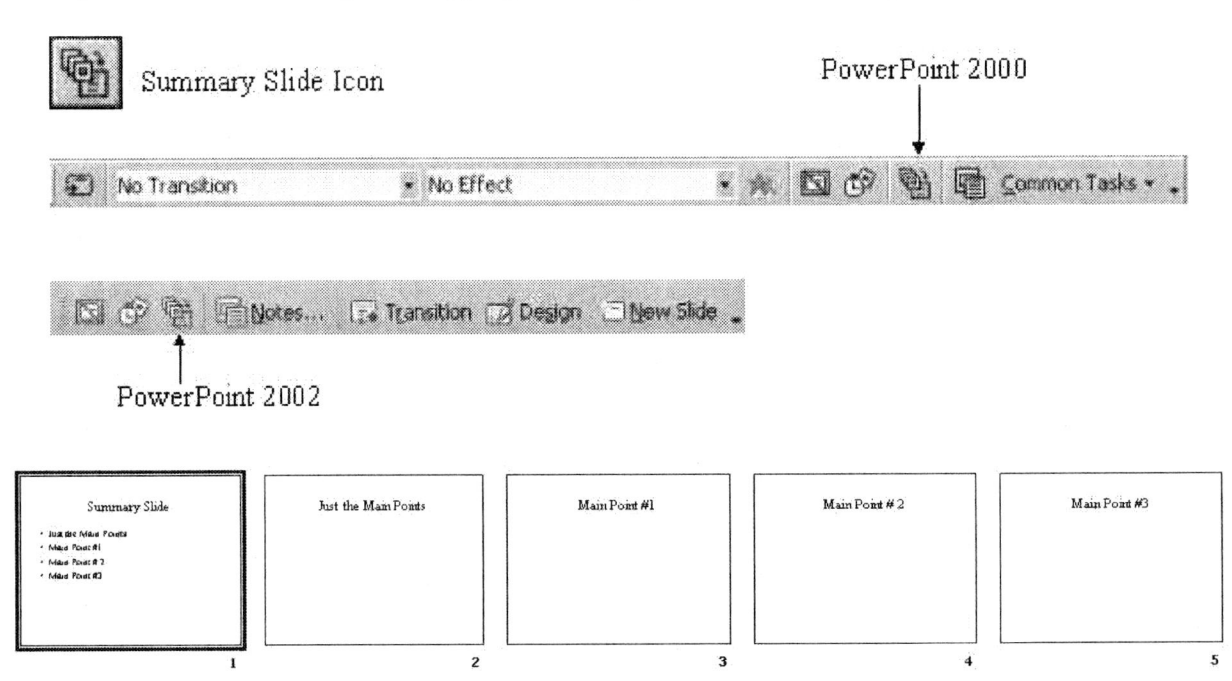

 **Tip: Panes are not Painful**

PowerPoint 2002 users will enjoy the addition of task panes to the program. Task panes are located on the far right of the screen, nestled under the Standard and Formatting toolbar areas. Great for visual learners, these special panes make working on slides a snap. Check to see that they are "turned on" by looking for a checkmark next to **Task Pane** in the **View** menu. The name of each pane appears in the Task pane title bar area.

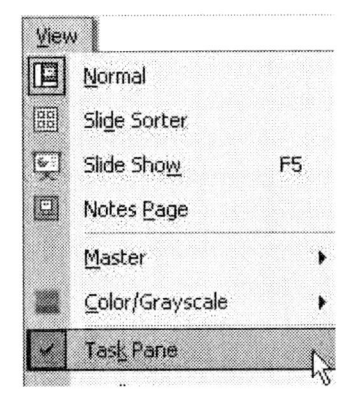 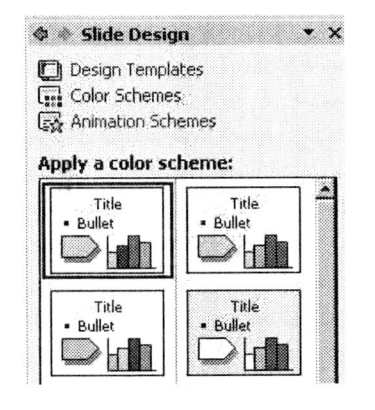

 **Trick: Save the Fonts**

If you are fond of using exotic fonts for the text on your slides, remember that they may not be present on the computer you will use to show your presentation. Some fonts, like Times New Roman or Arial, can be found on most computers. This is why these are the default fonts in a new presentation.

To be sure that your font is always available you'll need to *embed* it into your presentation. (Note that this only works with TrueType fonts and it **will** increase the file size of your completed presentation). *PowerPoint 2000* users can embed the fonts by clicking the **File** menu, selecting **Save As**, and choosing **Tools**. Next choose **Embed TrueType Fonts**. Name and save your presentation as usual.

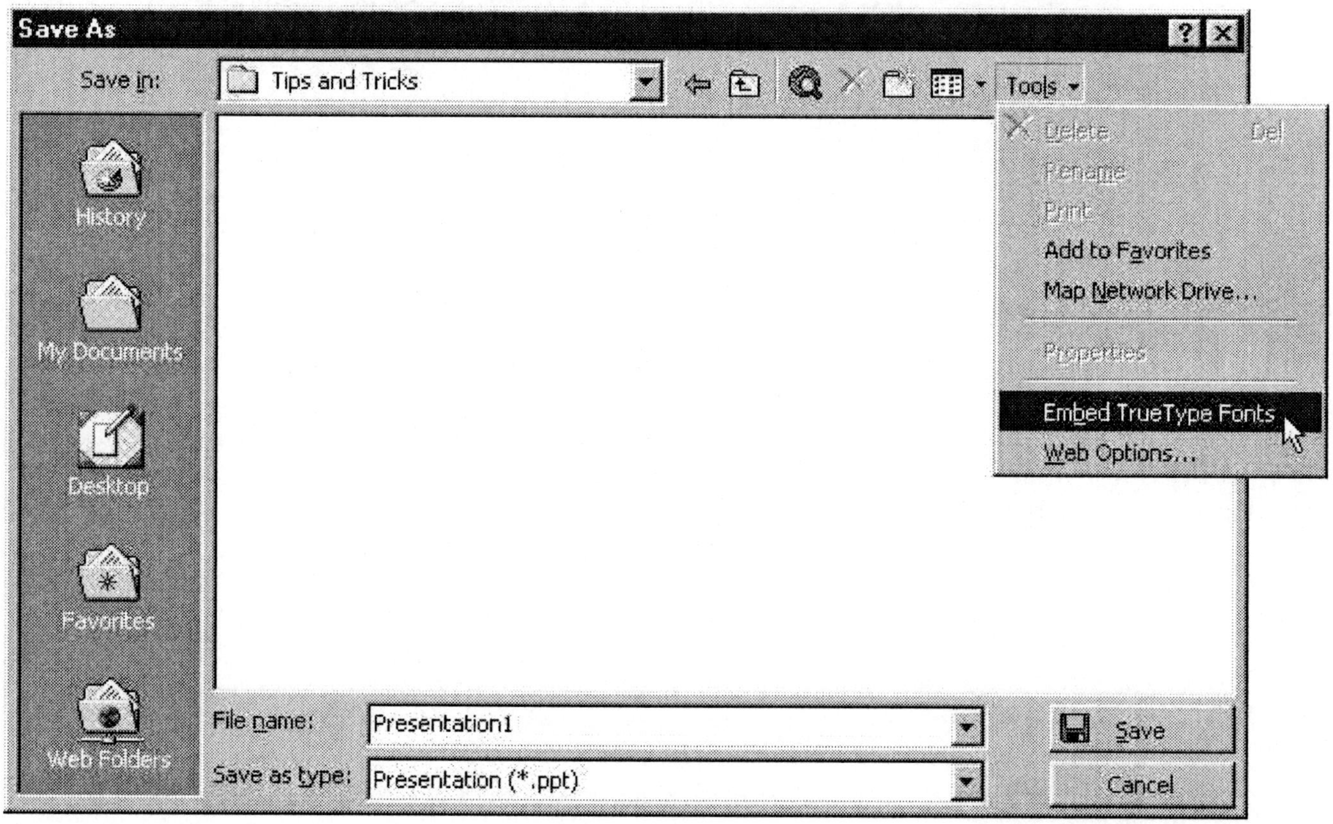

In *PowerPoint* 2002, embed fonts by first clicking the **Tools** menu and choosing **Options**. Next, click on the **Save** tab and choose **Embed TrueType** fonts. Then click to select the button next to **Embed all characters**. Although it creates a document with a larger file size, this option will allow you to make changes while you are in the field.

This embedding process is for the current document only, so if you have other presentations that need this font, you will have to repeat this process for each one. Remember, use caution when picking a fancy font. The font you choose will need to be readable at a distance. Keep in mind that special fonts can be purchased for typing math and science equations and foreign languages.

Tip: Font Substitution

If you wish to replace one font with another throughout a presentation, first choose **Format** then **Replace Fonts**. In the **Replace:** field, select the font you wish to change and in the **With:** field, choose the new font you wish to use. Click **Replace**. Repeat this procedure to replace other fonts. This tip can come in handy if you forgot to embed your fonts in the presentation and have to substitute other ones in a hurry!

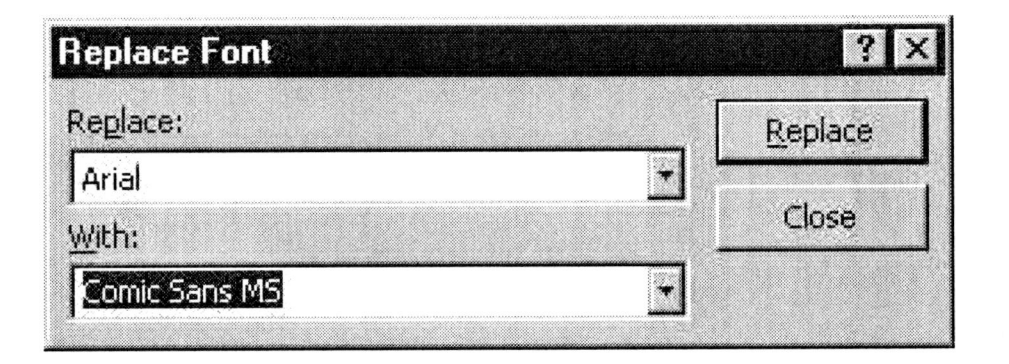

Tip: Special Ways with Fonts

Use the Font dialog box to apply special formatting to selected text on your slides. For example, you may need to use superscript or subscript. Select the text that needs to be formatted, then click the **Format** menu and choose **Font**. Choose the effect you want. To see how it will look on your slide, click the **Preview** button before clicking **OK**. Although fancy fonts may be fun, consider how they will look during a presentation or in the handouts of your slides.

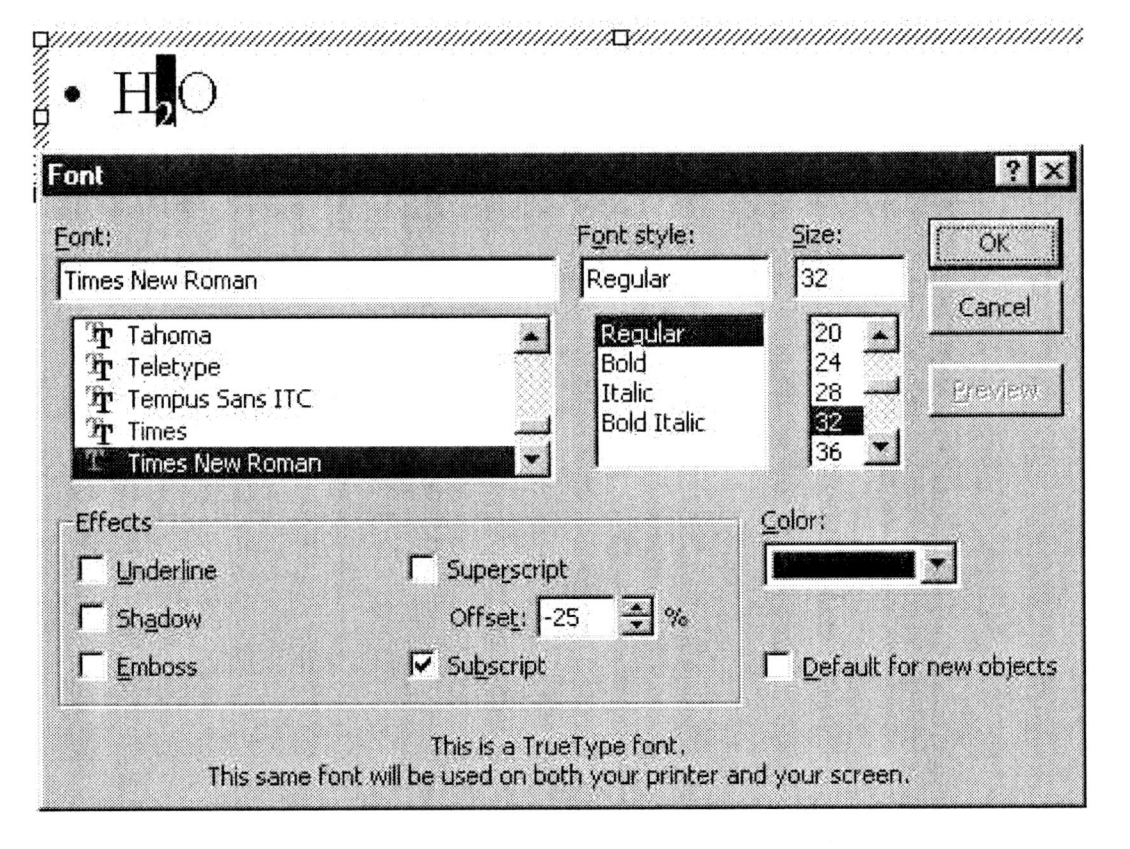

Trick: Don't Underline!

The Font dialog box contains an underline option that you shouldn't use routinely. If you are looking to underline text in a title placeholder, draw a line under it instead of using the underline feature. Underlining is a commonly used method to indicate a hyperlink; your audience may be confused by your underlined text and think it is a Web address (URL). Finally, the underlined text may be unreadable at a distance.

Don't Underline!

- <u>yyyyyyy</u>
- <u>Underlined text can be difficult to read.</u>

Tip: Use Format Painter

Save yourself a lot of time by learning about the Format Painter feature. The job of this tool is to copy all of the formatting (font style, size, bold, color, effects, etc.) of selected text and quickly apply it to other text on the same slide or on other slides in your presentation. You can also use Format Painter to copy carefully applied formatting from one object to other objects.

To use Format Painter with text, first apply your desired formatting to the text in your title or body text placeholders. Then select the text and click the **Format Painter** icon on the **Standard** toolbar. The cursor will change to a paintbrush. Place the paintbrush on the text to which you want to apply the formatting and click. Instantly, your text will be changed to the desired formatting.

Apply formatting to multiple objects and text by double-clicking the **Format Painter** icon. This will allow you to apply formatting in more than one place. Release Format Painter by pressing the **ESC** key on the keyboard or by clicking on the **Format Painter** icon on the toolbar.

Tip: Get Around

Here are some useful keyboard shortcuts to move around within your presentation during the slide creation process. (Note: Make sure there are no placeholders or objects selected.)

- To move up one slide, press the **Page Up** key.
- To move down one slide, press the **Page Down** key.
- To move to the first slide, press **Ctrl-Home**.
- To move to the last slide, press **Ctrl-End**.

You can also move through a presentation by using the arrows on the keyboard or the scroll box on the scroll bar.

Useful and Easy PowerPoint Art

Not artistic? Use the Drawing toolbar to create very professional-looking effects in a matter of minutes (it's lots of fun, too!).

 **Tip: Objects Are Everything**

Experiment on a blank slide when learning to create art effects. Delete the slide when you are done and no one will see the result of your experimentation.

Things drawn on slides are called *objects* no matter what their size and shape. You manipulate objects when they are selected, that is, when the selection handles are showing.

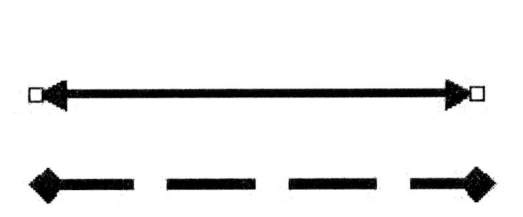

 **Tip: Show the Drawing Toolbar**

To create objects on your slides, you'll need to use the Drawing toolbar. If it is visible, it will most likely be at the bottom of the screen. If it isn't visible, turn it on by first selecting **Toolbars** from the **View** menu. A list of toolbars will appear. You will notice that the visible toolbars have checkmarks next to their names. Click the name of the toolbar you would like to have visible and a checkmark will appear. When you exit the menu, the toolbar will show up on your screen.

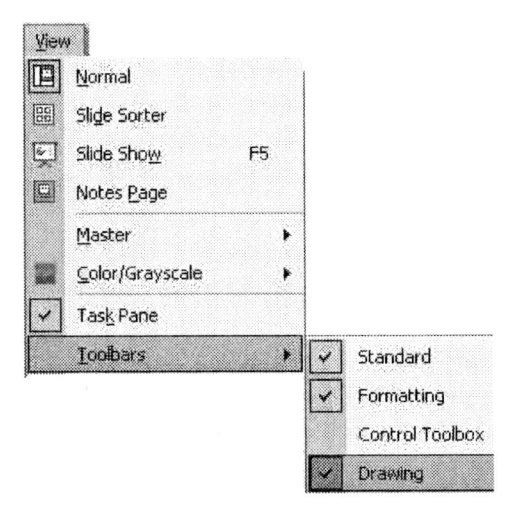

 ## Tip: Straight Lines and Arrowheads

Draw straight lines on your *PowerPoint* slides easily by holding down the **Shift** key while dragging to create a new line. To change the line thickness, first click the **Line Style** icon on the **Drawing** toolbar. From the pop-up menu, choose a line size. To select a color for the line, click on the **Line Color** icon and choose a color. You can create dashed lines with the **Dash Style** icon.

Lines that have arrow ends are created the same way using the Arrow tool. First click on the **Arrow** icon and draw your line. With the arrow line selected, click on the **Arrow Style** tool and select a style from the list. If you need a straight arrow, hold down the **Shift** key while drawing. Arrow lines can also be colored by using the Line Color icon.

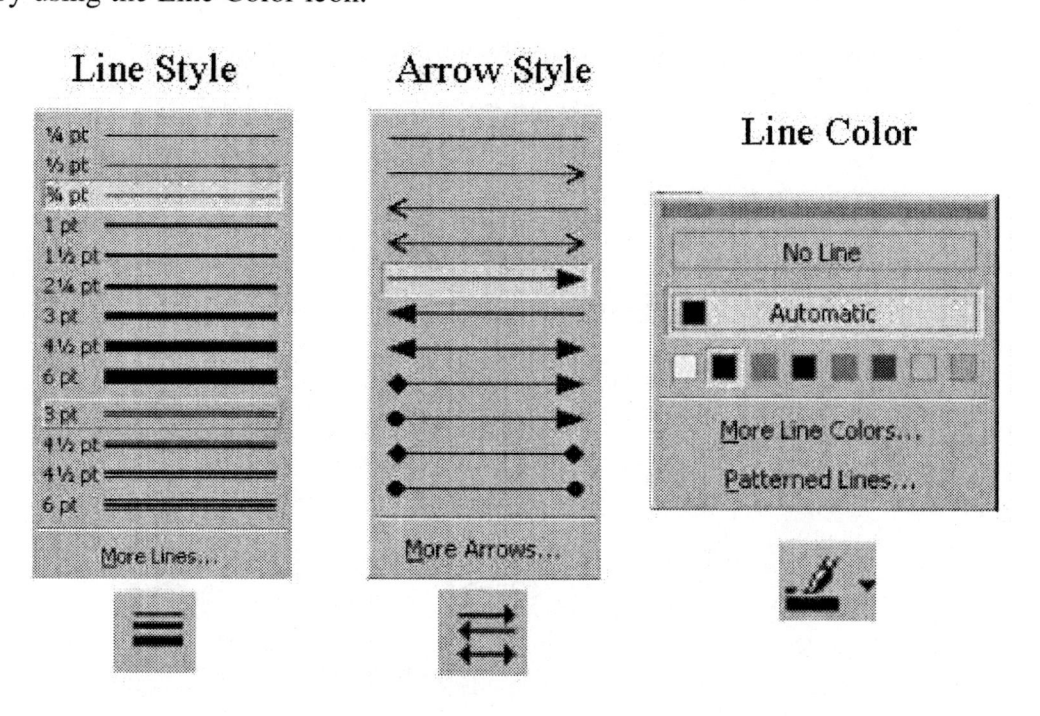

 ## Tip: Duplicate and Drag-Duplicate

Duplicate a line by selecting it, and then pressing **Ctrl-D**.

Create a "Rip-off" of a selected object by holding down the **Ctrl** key and dragging as if you were ripping the second copy away from the first. Once you get the hang of this technique you'll find a lot of uses for it. (This works with clip art and digital images too!)

Trick: Multiple Attributes

It's fairly tedious and time-consuming to change multiple attributes on a single line or arrowhead, so try this trick. Select the line. Click the **Format** menu and choose **AutoShape**. Set all of the style and color options at once using this dialog box.

Note: This trick can be used with any object drawn with the Draw tools on the Drawing toolbar.

 ## Tip: Oval or Circle, Rectangle or Square

Next to the line and arrow tools on the Drawing Toolbar are the oval and rectangle tools. After drawing an oval or rectangle on your slide, select it and use the Format AutoShapes feature to set the outline width. To do this, in the **Format AutoShapes** dialog box, select the **Colors and Lines** tab, then choose **Fill Color**. Use the **No Fill** option to make the shape empty.

Create perfect circles instead of ovals by holding down the **Shift** key while drawing with the **Oval** tool. Make perfect squares by pressing the **Shift** key while drawing with the **Rectangle** tool. Now try holding down the **Ctrl** key while drawing. Notice that the shape is drawn from the center out. Finally, press both the **Ctrl** and **Shift** keys while drawing and see what happens.

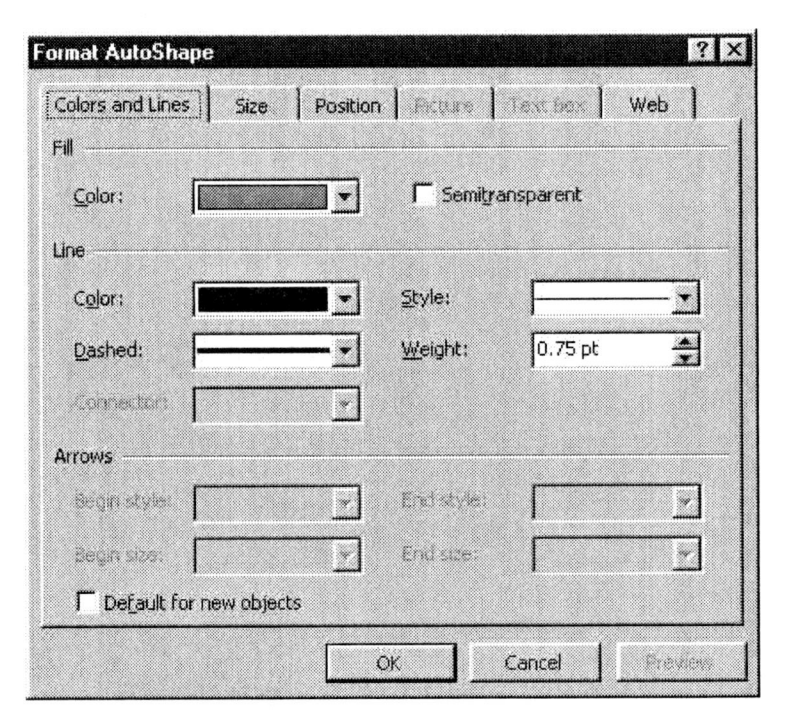

 ## Idea: Venn Diagram Graphic Organizer

On a blank slide, use the tips you just learned to create a circle with no fill. Select the circle and duplicate it. Drag the second circle to overlap the first, thus creating a Venn diagram. Select both circles with **Ctrl-A**. On the **Drawing** toolbar, click the word **Draw**, then choose **Align or Distribute**, and then **Align Top**.

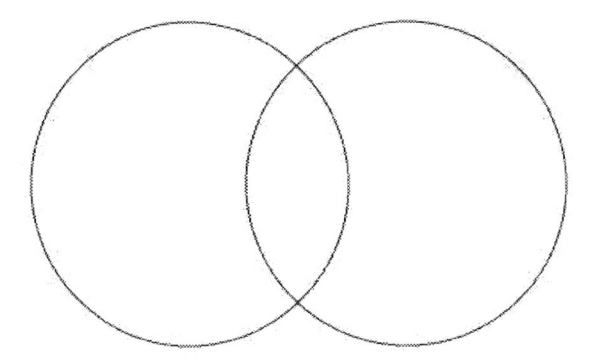

Putting Graphics to Work

Tip: AutoShapes Save Time

Instead of spending time looking for just the right graphic, take a look at the myriad of shapes that are available to you in the AutoShapes menu on the Drawing toolbar. (Remember, if you don't see the Drawing toolbar at the bottom of your screen, click the **View** menu, choose **Toolbars** and make sure there is a checkmark next to **Drawing**.) With the Drawing toolbar visible, click on **AutoShapes** to examine the categories of graphic objects like **Basic Shapes** and **Stars and Banners**. These useful shapes can be resized and reshaped to make dynamic objects for your slides.

Trick: Tear Off the Palette

Several menus on the Drawing toolbar can be ripped off from the toolbar to become floating palettes. Palettes can be placed alongside your slides for quick access. As you click on a menu on the **Drawing** toolbar, look for a tiny gray bar at the top. Hover your mouse pointer over this bar to see the ScreenTip message, "Drag to make this menu float." Press and drag this bar to temporarily remove or "rip off" the menu. This process transforms the pop-out menu into a floating palette with a tiny title bar and Close box. Drag the palette around on the screen by dragging the title bar. When you are finished with the palette, click the **Close** box on the palette's title bar to put it away. The palette will merge back with the menu.

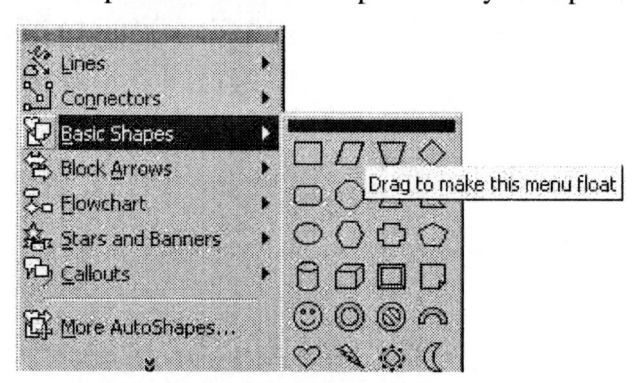

Idea: Classroom Award Certificates

Use a single slide to create an award certificate for your classroom that is easy to print and photocopy. Experiment with the lines, rectangles, and AutoShapes tools on the Drawing toolbar using this example as a guide.

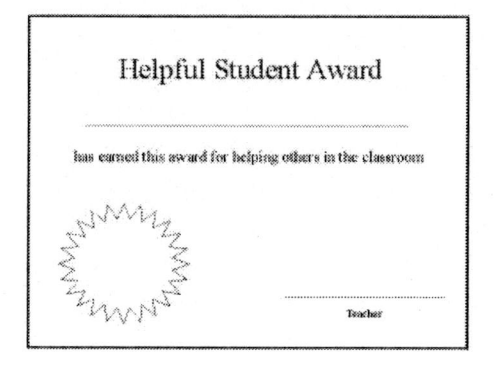

 ## Tip: The Holding Zone

The work area for slides can seem tight at times, so use the gray area around the slide as a parking spot for objects that you want to use but that are currently in the way. This area, the *pasteboard*, holds items for the current slide in use only. Items on the pasteboard won't print and won't be seen during a presentation. To see more of the pasteboard, resize the panes using the splitter bar.

 ## Tip: Measure Up

When working with graphic objects, it is useful to turn on the ruler. The ruler can help not only with the placement of objects on your slides, but it can also show you the size of objects created with the Drawing toolbar. To turn on the ruler, click the **View** menu and choose **Ruler**. A checkmark appears when the ruler is showing. Hide the ruler by choosing it again.

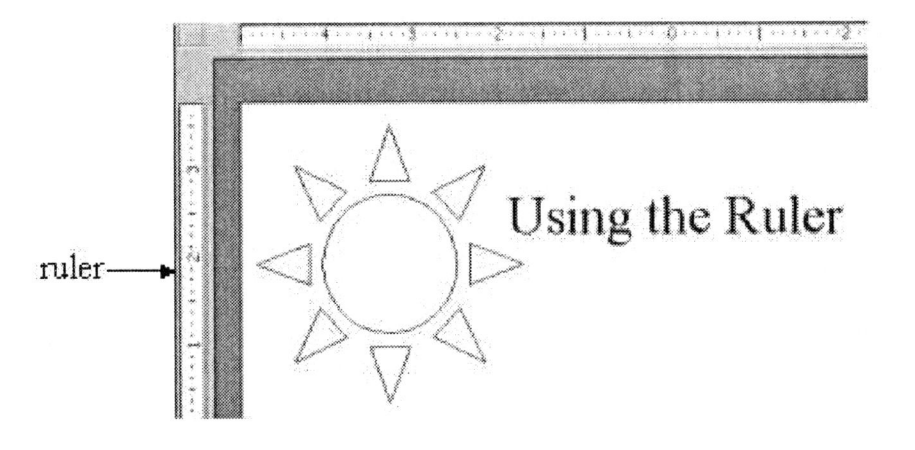

 ## Tip: Nudging

If you've ever wished you could move a selected object over just a little bit, then you need to learn about nudging. To nudge, select the object and then use the Drawing toolbar's **Nudge** command to move the object up, down, right, or left just a wee bit. Another way to do this is to hold down the **Ctrl** key while pressing the up, down, right, or left arrows on the keyboard.

 ## Tip: Ducks in a Row

Occasionally, you may need to align objects in a row. Place your first object on the slide, format it if needed, and select it. Make another object by holding down the **Ctrl** key and dragging to create an exact replica of the first object. Continue this process until you have the number of objects you need. Select all of the objects by clicking the first, then holding down the **Shift** key and clicking the next object in turn until all are selected. Then from the Drawing toolbar, click **Draw** and choose **Align or Distribute**. Choose the desired alignment and your objects will align themselves. Made a mistake? Press **Ctrl-Z** to undo the alignment and then try another. To make "ducks in a row," choose **Align Top** and the top edge of the objects will be neatly aligned. Note: you can ensure they will stay aligned by grouping them. To do this, click **Draw** on the **Drawing** toolbar and choose **Group**.

 ## Tricks: Arrays and Sweeps

An array is a series of evenly spaced (horizontal or vertical) objects, and a sweep is a series of evenly spaced objects that overlap slightly. The definitions and instructions for creating these object "special effects" are nestled in the Help file of *PowerPoint 2000*.

To create an array, select the object, click the **Edit** menu, and choose **Duplicate**. Drag the copied object to the position you want, then click the **Edit** menu and choose **Duplicate**. You can continue duplicating by pressing **Ctrl-D** until you have all the desired objects.

Making a sweep is easy too! To make a sweep, select the object to be duplicated. Click the **Edit** menu and choose **Copy**. Then click the **Edit** menu and choose **Paste**. The copied object will slightly overlap the first object. Continue pasting until you have finished your sweep. As a shortcut, the keyboard command **Ctrl-V** will repeat your paste command.

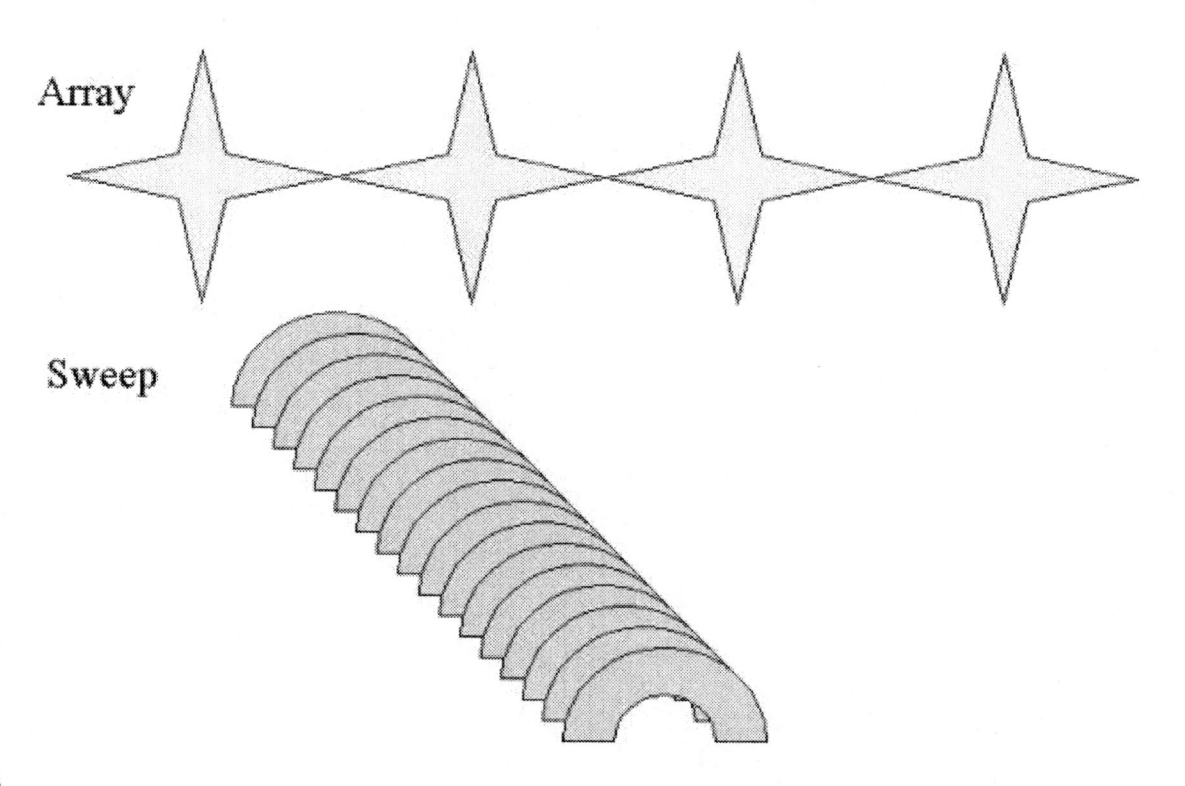

Array

Sweep

 ## Tip: The Picture Toolbar

A versatile toolbar to have at your fingertips is the Picture toolbar. This toolbar is handy for altering certain kinds of images such as the graphics in the Clip Art Gallery. It isn't usually showing so you'll have to turn it on by clicking the **View** menu and choosing **Picture** from the list of toolbars. The Picture toolbar is a floating toolbar by default so you'll need to drag it around by its title bar as needed. Experiment by inserting a graphic from the Clip Art Gallery and then use the tools such as Contrast, Brightness and Grayscale to enhance and alter the image.

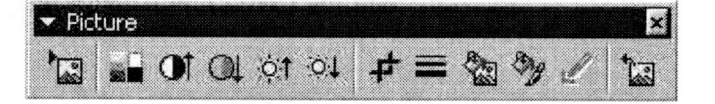

 **Tip: Only the Shadow Knows**

Adding a shadow effect to a graphic can make a simple image seem very dramatic, especially if it is a grayscale or black and white photograph. To create a shadow, first outline your graphic or digital image with a line. To do this, first click on your graphic to select it. Then click the **Line Style** icon on the **Drawing** toolbar. Choose a line thickness suitable for your image. When you are satisfied with the effect, locate the **Shadow** icon on the **Drawing** toolbar and apply a shadow style. Use the **Shadow Setting** option to add a colored shadow.

 **Trick: Export a Slide to a Graphic**

If you have made a spectacular slide (or slides) and you would like to save it as a graphic to be used in other applications, you can! Be sure you have saved the slide or slides as a regular presentation first in case you decide to modify the slide later. Then click the **File** menu and choose **Save As**. Name and save your presentation as you normally do. Now click the **File** menu and choose **Save As** again. This time, click the **Save as type** drop-down box and choose **JPEG File Interchange Format**. Name your graphic, navigate to a saving location, and click the **Save** button. (Note: you will have the choice of saving the current slide or more than one slide depending on what you have created.)

| File name: | Star | | 💾 Save |
| Save as type: | JPEG File Interchange Format (*.jpg) | | Cancel |

Trick: AutoShape Text and Fills

Filling an AutoShape with a picture of your own is a snap! To do this, first draw the AutoShape on your slide. (Note: Ignore the filled color because it will disappear when you fill it with your picture.) Then click on your newly drawn AutoShape to select it. On the **Drawing** toolbar, locate the **Fill** icon that looks like a paint bucket. Click on the tiny drop-down arrow next to the paint bucket and choose **Fill Effects**. The Fill Effects dialog box will open. Click the **Picture** tab. Next click the **Select Picture** button and navigate to the location where you have previously saved a graphic or picture that you wish to use. Select the graphic and the image will appear in the Picture area. This ensures that you have chosen the correct image. Now click **OK**. The AutoShape will be filled with your own graphic. Note: you can use the same procedure to fill an AutoShape with gradients, textures, or patterns.

Add text to your AutoShape by clicking to select the AutoShape and then just type! A text box will be created automatically. Use the tools on the Formatting toolbar or Formatting Task pane to change the font, style, color, and size.

Thinking of Printing?

 ## Trick: Don't Use the Print icon!

The Print icon on the Standard toolbar prints your slides in full size (8½" by 11") one after another and in full color when using a color printer. You can waste a lot of paper and color ink or toner this way! If that's what you need, fine, just click it. Otherwise, keep an open mind about printing by reading all the tips and tricks in this section.

 ## Tip: Avoid the Mud

Ink jet printers are a popular choice for home and classroom use because they are inexpensive to purchase. Think ahead! Are you planning to print out your presentation, photocopy it, and hand it out? Color printouts make for muddy or completely black graphics when reproduced by photocopying. If you'd like to conserve the color printer ink or are using a black and white laser printer, take a look at your slides before printing by using the handy **Grayscale Preview** icon on the **Standard** toolbar. This feature doesn't change your slides; it just allows them to be viewed in shades of gray. This will give you an idea of how your handouts will look.

PowerPoint 2002 users have more options. To see these options, click the **View** menu, choose **Color/Grayscale**, then **Grayscale** to show the Grayscale View dialog box. Use the **Settings** drop-down box to view your slides in multiple shades of gray.

Just because you can *view* your presentation in grayscale doesn't mean it will print in grayscale. To print your color slides in grayscale you need to click the **File** menu and choose **Print**. Select the print options you desire. Users of *PowerPoint* 2002 can view their slides before printing by using **Print Preview** in the **File** menu.

 ## Tip: Accept a Handout

Examine the options for printing handouts in the Print what: section of the Print dialog box. To access this, make sure the presentation is open, then click the **File** menu and choose **Print**. Click the **Print what:** drop-down box to see that the choices are Slides, Handouts, Notes pages, and Outline view. Choose **Handouts**. In the Handouts section, click the drop-down box next to **Slides per page** to see the choices 1, 2, 3, 4, 6, and 9 slides per page. These can be arranged in a horizontal or vertical pattern. Notice the sample view of your choices to help you visualize how the slides will look.

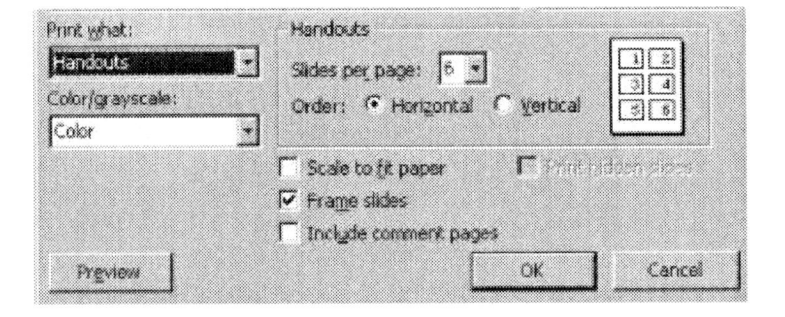

If you have a lot of small text on your slides that must be readable on your handouts, you may have to use the option of 2 or 3 slides. A favorite choice of teachers is three slides per page because it places lines for taking notes to the right of each slide.

 **Tip: Kinds of Printouts**

As you are creating your slides, you should be "scripting" what you are going to say during the presentation. Jot notes down in the **Notes** area while you create your slides. Formerly called Speaker Notes, this small area is handy for recording those brilliant things you wish to say. Later on you can access your notes by clicking the **View** menu and selecting your **Notes pages**. In this view, each slide is shown along with whatever notes you hastily jotted down. Click in the text area, adjust the view with the **Zoom** box on the **Standard** toolbar, and re-work those ideas into the witty, informative material you are going to present.

Print each one of these Notes pages to have handy as you are practicing your presentation. To do this, click the **File** menu, choose **Print**, and in the **Print What:** area, choose **Notes Pages**. The resulting printout will be an enlarged slide with your text underneath it. Note that only a certain amount of text can be added to this page.

Outlines can be printed too. For those students working in groups to develop a presentation, it is useful for each student to have a copy of the outline to help them develop their speech. This is a good alternative to having a printout of each slide, and it will save classroom toner/ink and paper. To print in outline form, click the **File** menu, choose **Print**, and in the **Print What:** area, choose **Outline View**.

 **Idea: Overhead Transparencies**

Many classrooms and schools have a single projection device which must be shared among all the teachers. If you have created a *PowerPoint* presentation and the projection device is not available, consider purchasing some ink jet or laser printer overhead transparency film. You can print each slide on a transparency and use them on the more readily available overhead projector. To print on transparencies, click the **File** menu and choose **Page Setup**. Click the **Slides sized for:** drop-down box and choose **Overhead**. Then print the currently selected slide by clicking the **File** menu, choosing **Print**, and in the **Print Range** section, choosing **Current Slide**. (By the way, be sure you are using the correct transparency film for your printer. Laser transparency film is special in that it will not melt with the heat of laser printing. Ink jet film is right for printing with color ink.)

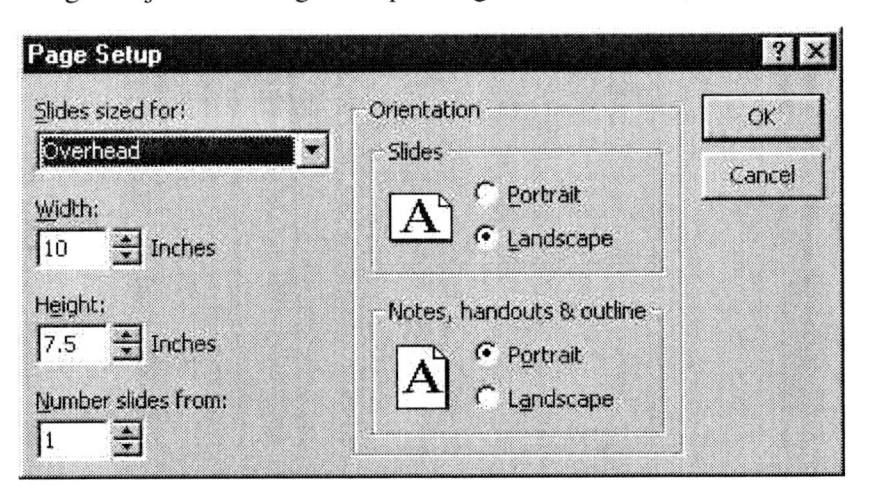

 **Tip: Make a Storyboard**

To allow students to draft their own presentations, create a "blank slide" presentation with three empty slides. Print it as a three-slide handout with lines to use as a graphic organizer or storyboard. Students can sketch out their slides in the blank slide areas, and jot down notes for each slide on this storyboard.

 ## Trick: Send it to Word

For more control over your printouts, *PowerPoint* presentations can be sent to Word where you can add your own touches. (Note that this doesn't change your slides in any way.) In Word, you can add headers and footers such as your name, the date, school name, and page numbers. This feature is most useful for writing up your full presentation for a stress-free delivery day or an emergency fill-in presenter.

Further, the slides are placed inside a table, so if you know how to work with tables in Word, your choices are endless. A final reason to bring your slides into a Word document is to share a presentation with a fellow colleague or student who doesn't have *PowerPoint* but has Word.

To send your files to Word, first click the **File** menu, choose **Send to**, and then choose **Microsoft Word**. The **Writeup** or **Send to Microsoft Word** dialog box appears, where you must choose a style of layout for your presentation to be formatted in Word. Note: sending your presentation to Word creates a large file so don't plan to save it on a floppy.

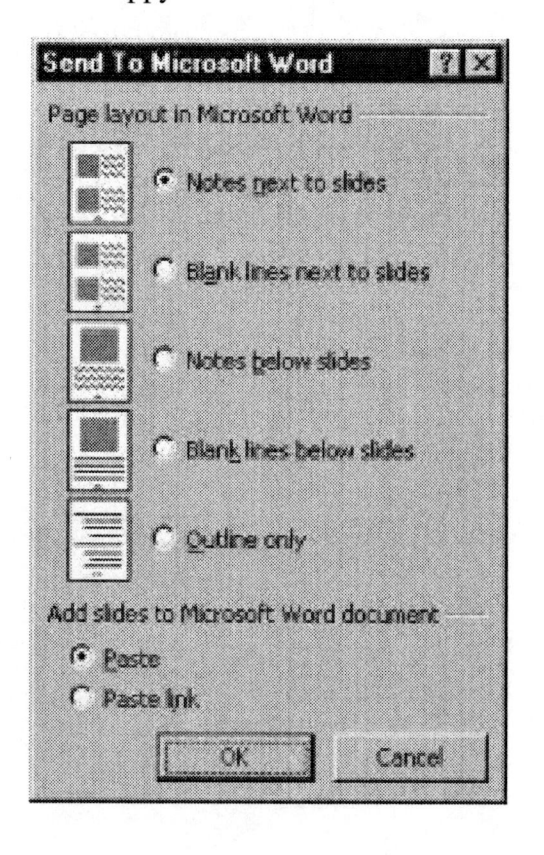

Fast Learning for Teachers

Trick: What's This?

If you want to get a quick answer about the function of an icon on a toolbar or to understand an option in a dialog box, you can press **Shift** and the **F1** keys together to turn on the "**What's This?**" help feature. When these two keys are pressed together, the cursor changes to a large question mark. Use this cursor to click on the icon or option you'd like to know more about and a box will appear with an explanation or definition. Click outside the box when you have read the explanation to exit this special feature. You can also access this feature by clicking the **?** box if it is available in the upper right-hand corner of the dialog box.

Also, right-clicking with your mouse on most areas and buttons in a dialog box will bring you context-sensitive "**What's This?**" help for the area you right-clicked.

Tip: Useful Keyboard Shortcuts

It's not hard to find useful keyboard shortcuts for *PowerPoint*. Try searching in *PowerPoint* **Help** for "**keyboard shortcuts**." You can also use Microsoft's Web site pages for your version of *PowerPoint* to find printable lists. Many keyboard shortcuts you have learned for Microsoft Word will work too, especially for text in placeholders. For those cross-platform users of both *PowerPoint* for Windows and Macintosh, be aware that not all keyboard shortcuts work the same way on both platforms.

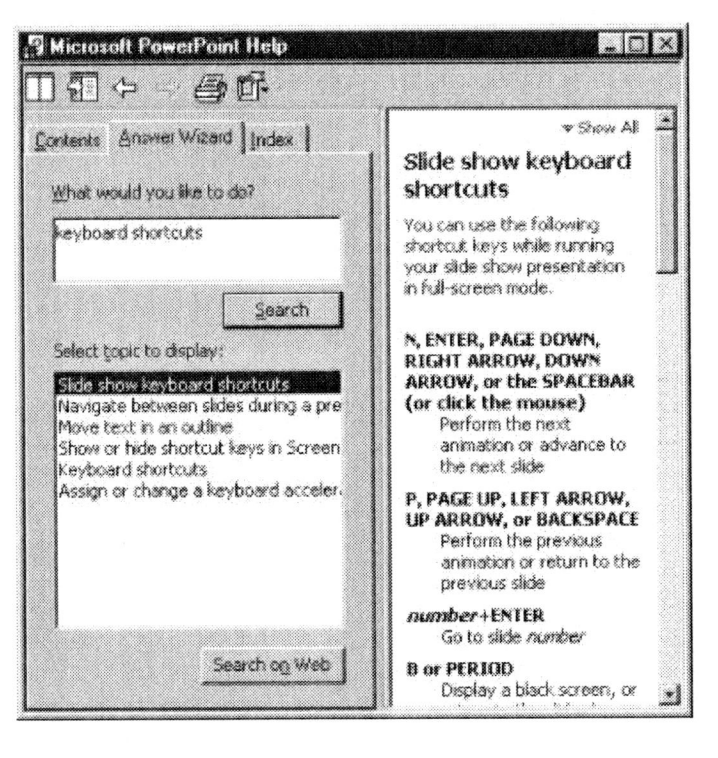

Jazzing it Up!

Before venturing into the wonderful world of multimedia, it is wise to pause and think about providing your audience or classroom with solid content, well-designed slides, and a powerfully-built plan of delivery. When working with students on presentations, mentoring students in these areas is essential. When it comes to adding "bells and whistles," students will swiftly grasp using transitions, animations, sounds, and movies. Each new version of *PowerPoint* adds yet more special effects, so there's always more to learn.

 ## Tip: Resist Transition Temptation

Transitions are effects that occur as you move from one slide to the next slide. Transitions should be used to visually guide your audience's attention from one slide to another. Pick one transition to use with all of the slides in your presentation. Avoid headaches; decide on a transition and use it consistently in each presentation.

 ## Tip: Just Passing Through

Transitions are best applied using the Slide Sorter view. When a transition is applied to a slide, a transition icon appears below it. This visual helps you easily identify which slides have transitions and which don't.

To apply the same transition to all slides, click the **Edit** menu and choose **Select All**. (Note: the selected slides will have a heavy outline box around them.) *PowerPoint 2000* users will see the **Slide Sorter** toolbar appear. Select a transition from the drop-down list. *PowerPoint* 2002 users will see a button named **Transition** on the **Slide Sorter** toolbar. When it is clicked the **Slide Transition** task pane will open, and a list of transitions will appear. After applying a transition, click on the icon that appears below the slide to "play" the transition so you can see how it works with your presentation.

The speed of how a transition plays can be important. Applied transitions are supposed to catch the audience's attention without mesmerizing them. To adjust the speed of a transition, *PowerPoint 2000* users can open the **Slide Transition** dialog box from the **Slide Sorter** toolbar (or click the **Slide Show** menu, then choose **Slide Transition**). *PowerPoint* 2002 users can adjust speed using the **Slide Transition** task pane. Remember, slow, medium, or fast speeds are quite subjective as computers vary in power. A more powerful computer will allow for faster transitions. Think of slower computers or slides heavy in graphics as speed bumps.

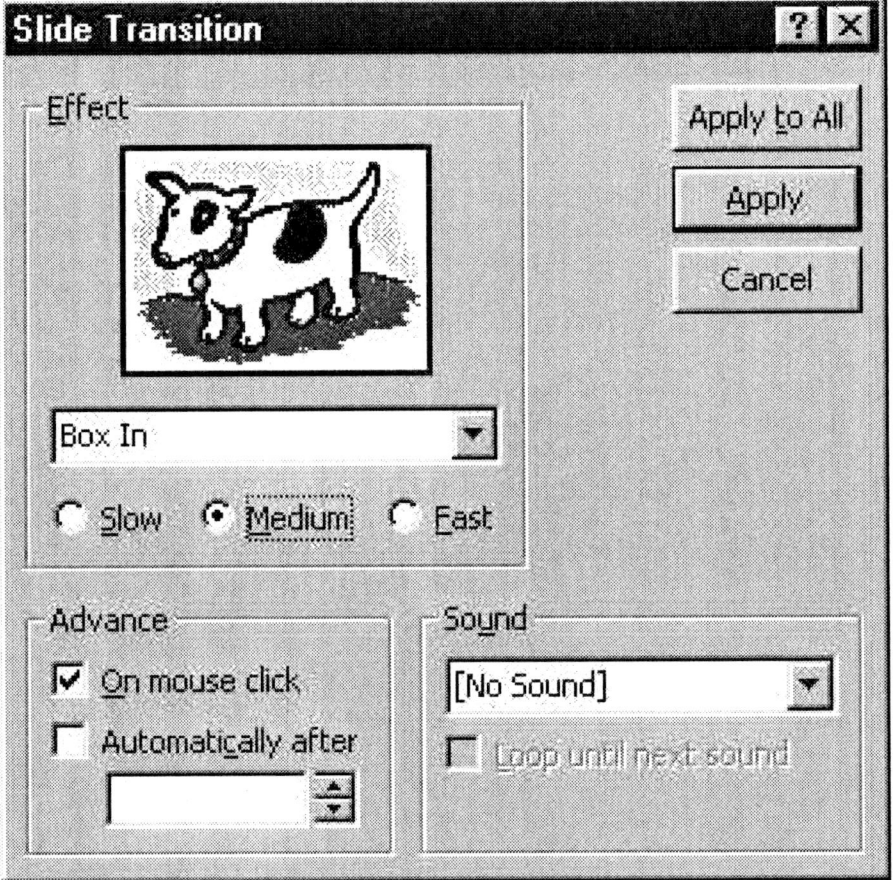

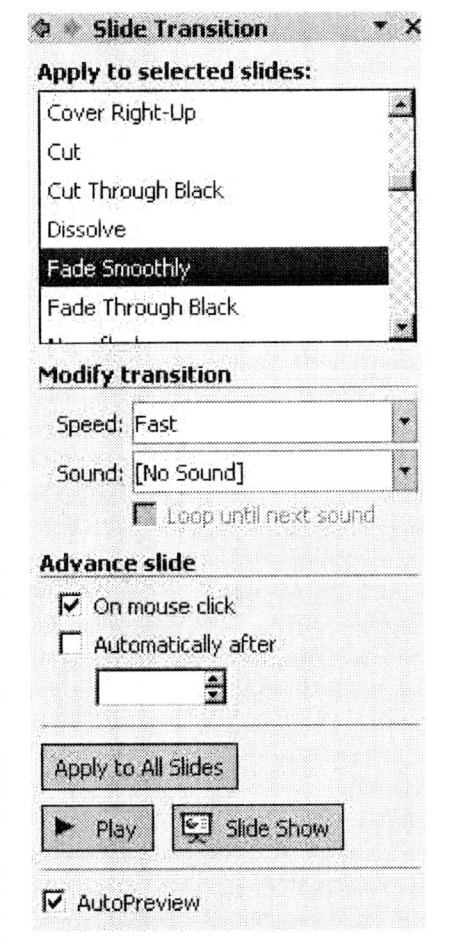

 **Trick: Dysfunctional Transitions**

Have students create a four-slide presentation on a topic they know well. Assign each student a transition or two to use consistently in their mini-presentation. Ask each student to write a description of the transition's action (the transition name can help in this). Ask students if the speed improves or detracts from the transition. Make a classroom list of the purposes and critiques of the transitions.

Trick: Teachers in Control

Build "effective use of multimedia" into the rubrics used to assess student presentations. Also, because of limited classroom time for presenting slide shows, decide how many transitions and animations students will use *before* they create their slides.

Tip: EZ Animation

Use Preset Animations or Animation schemes to do quick animations of graphic objects and text placeholders on your slides. *PowerPoint* animation is the term used to describe how an object or a group of text appears on a slide. Some of these "pre-packaged" groups of effects are for graphics and some are for text. Depending on what you have selected—text or graphic—the available animations will be displayed.

PowerPoint 2000 users can apply a preset animation scheme in Normal or Slide Sorter View. For Normal view, click the text or select the graphic object you wish to animate. Click the **Slide Show** menu and choose **Preset Animation**. The preset animations appear in the sub-menu. Be sure to notice that the first choice is OFF. If you decide to remove an animation, you will need to return here to turn it off. In Slide Sorter View, apply a preset animation from the **Slide Sorter** toolbar. For power users, there is a handy Animation toolbar. Use it by first clicking the **View** menu, then choosing **Toolbars** and finally, selecting **Animation Effects Toolbar**.

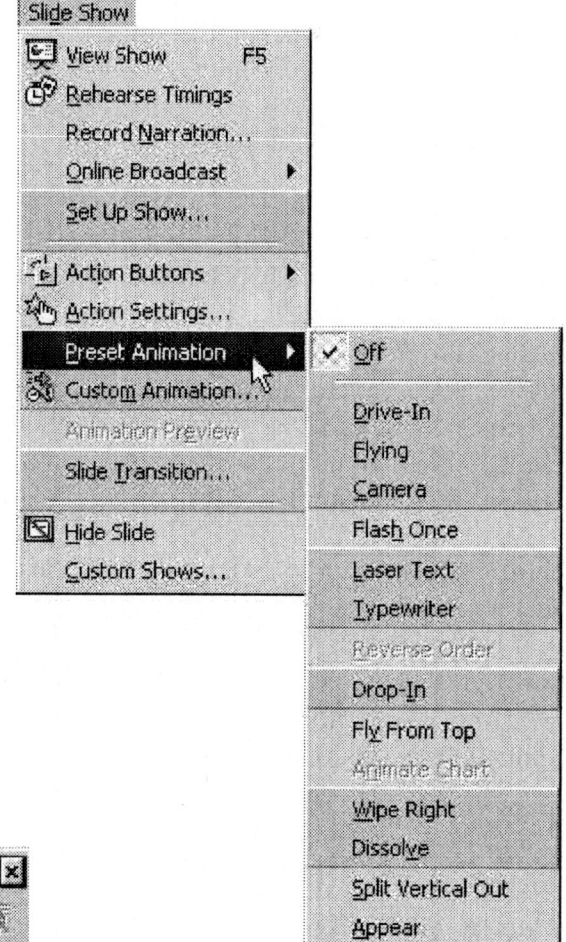

PowerPoint 2002 users can use the Slide Design task pane to simplify the process of adding animation schemes. From the **Slide Show** menu, choose **Animation Schemes**. Alternatively, click the **Design** button on the **Formatting** toolbar to bring up the **Slide Design** task pane. Click on the subsection **Animation Schemes** to see the list of effects. These groups of effects are listed in three categories: Subtle, Moderate, and Exciting. There is also an effect called No Animation that can be used to remove an applied animation.

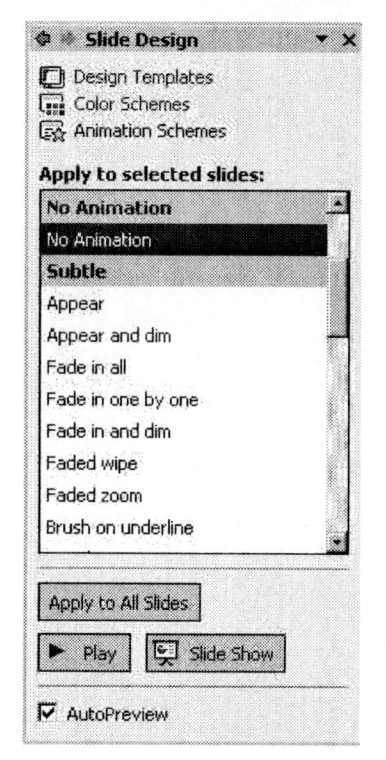

After applying text/object animations to slides, be sure to run your presentation to see the full effect. If you applied your effect in Normal view, running the presentation is the only way to see the animation. In **Slide Sorter** view, click the small icon under each slide that indicates an applied animation to play the animation. *PowerPoint* 2002 users can click **Play** in the **Slide Design** task pane to see animations on each slide. Always run the entire show to see the complete effect of the animations.

 ## Tip: Building Text Animations

Somehow, dancing alphabets come to mind when thinking of animated text! Early versions of *PowerPoint* called the process of animating text "building the text," and it has long been a staple of business users of *PowerPoint*. Designed to be suspenseful, they are called builds because of their "one after another" appearance on the screen to build on previous comments or ideas. Preset or Animation schemes applied to text are for title and body placeholders only. Text is then treated as a group and is animated paragraph by paragraph (which may be bullet by bullet). The only way to animate text word-by-word or letter-by-letter is to create a Custom Animation.

Before applying these text animations consider what you will be saying while the text appears on the screen. If you are handing out your presentation in printed form to your class or audience prior to the presentation, most participants will have read what you were hoping would be suspenseful before they see it, thus ruining the effect. Also, it takes longer to present material one line at a time. Try one of the text animations on the first slide in your presentation to learn how to use them. Animations can be applied to text on one slide using Normal View or to one or all slides in Slide Sorter View.

 ## Trick: Use Animated GIFs

PowerPoint 2000 was the first version of *PowerPoint* for Windows to allow the use of animated GIFs. These graphics are pre-created in a special application and animate on their own without applying any animations from *PowerPoint*. Many are available for free on the Internet and there are some in the Clip Art Gallery. Note that animated GIFs won't "*move*" until you run the presentation.

 ## Tip: Effects of Custom Animation

If you'd like to exert more control over the animations you are using, then working with the Custom Animations of *PowerPoint* is right for you. It can take a lot of time to explore these special techniques so only a few will be covered here.

Many teachers enjoy the visual effects of the animations but dislike the screeching brakes, whooshing, and breaking glass sounds of which students are so fond. These sound effects can be silenced. If multiple animations have been applied to one slide, use the Custom Animation controls to decide which plays first. The best way to learn Customized Animations is to experiment with the options and decide which are best for you.

PowerPoint 2000 users can access the Custom Animation controls by selecting a slide to work with in **Normal** view, clicking the **Slide Show** menu, and choosing **Custom Animation**. The tabs in the Custom Animation dialog box allow you to manipulate the objects on this *currently selected* slide. In this tip, the Effects tab will be explored.

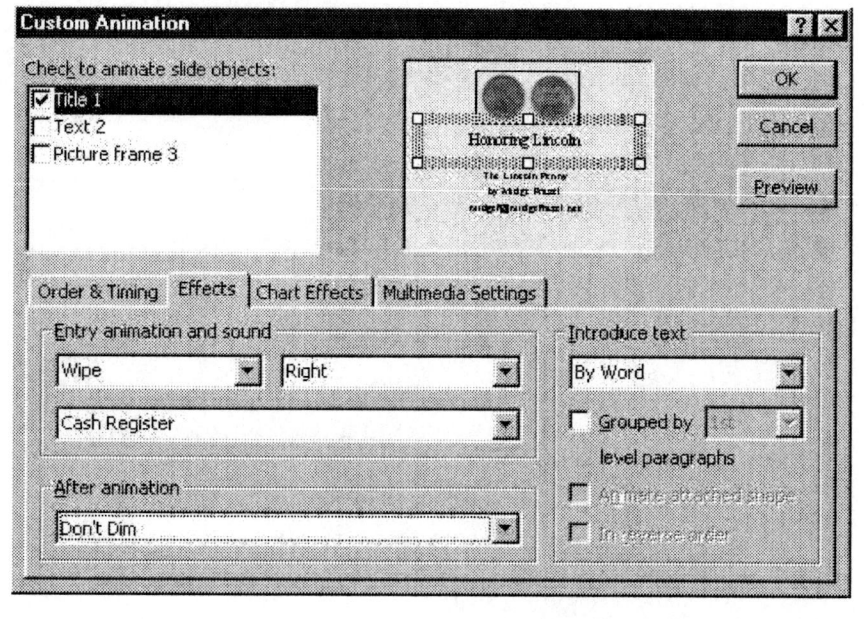

Use the settings under the **Effects** tab to decide which object(s) to animate with which effect. First, select the object in the **Check to animate slide objects** section in the upper left-hand corner by clicking a checkmark next to the name of the object. Use the Preview box to the right to see that you have chosen the correct object.

In the **Entry animation and sound** section, first choose an animation effect from the drop-down box. When you choose one, its direction of entry will appear. If it has a sound effect applied to it that will appear too. If the object is text, then you can use the **Introduce Text** section to adjust the arrival of text all at once, by word, or by letter. Remember, the default is **all at once**. In the **After Animation** section, choose what will happen on your slide when the animation(s) is finished. This is similar to a transition.

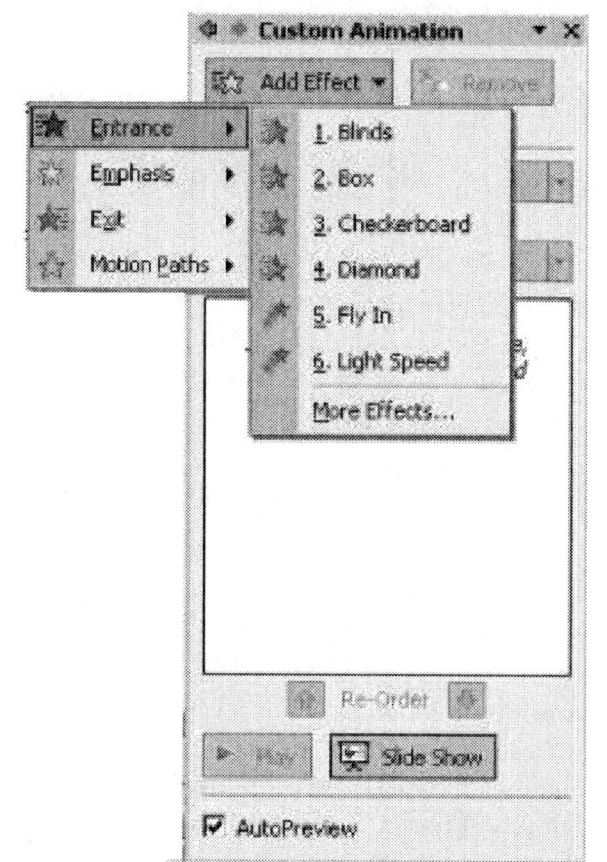

If you are a *PowerPoint 2002* user, you can access the Custom Animation controls by first selecting a slide to work with in **Normal** view. Then click the **Slide Show** menu and choose **Custom Animation**. This opens the Custom Animation task pane. On your slide, select the object to which you wish to add an animation. Choose animation schemes under the **Add Effects** drop-down menu. Once you select an effect, it will play if there is a checkmark next to **AutoPreview**. The applied effects can be further manipulated with options in the Custom Animation task pane. Be sure to notice the Remove button, which allows you to remove unwanted applied animations.

Presentable Presentations

 **Tip: Presentation Types**

Most of the time, *PowerPoint* presentations are designed to be "instructor-led." Teachers find *PowerPoint* presentations are effective for sharing information with students in a direct manner. In addition, student projects created and presented by a team of students is an equally effective "instructor-led" model. But, there is another type of presentation that teachers and students can use: a "self-running" or kiosk presentation. Educators find many uses for this design, from tutorials for students who were absent, to open house presentations, to retirement and party-related shows.

 **Tip: Hands-Free Presentations**

To set up a kiosk presentation, first click the **Slide Show** menu and then choose **Set Up Show**. The Set Up Show dialog box appears. In the **Show type** section, click to select **Browsed at a kiosk**. This will set the screen show to fit the entire monitor screen. In the **Advance slides** section click to select the **Using timings, if present**. Click **OK** to exit this dialog box.

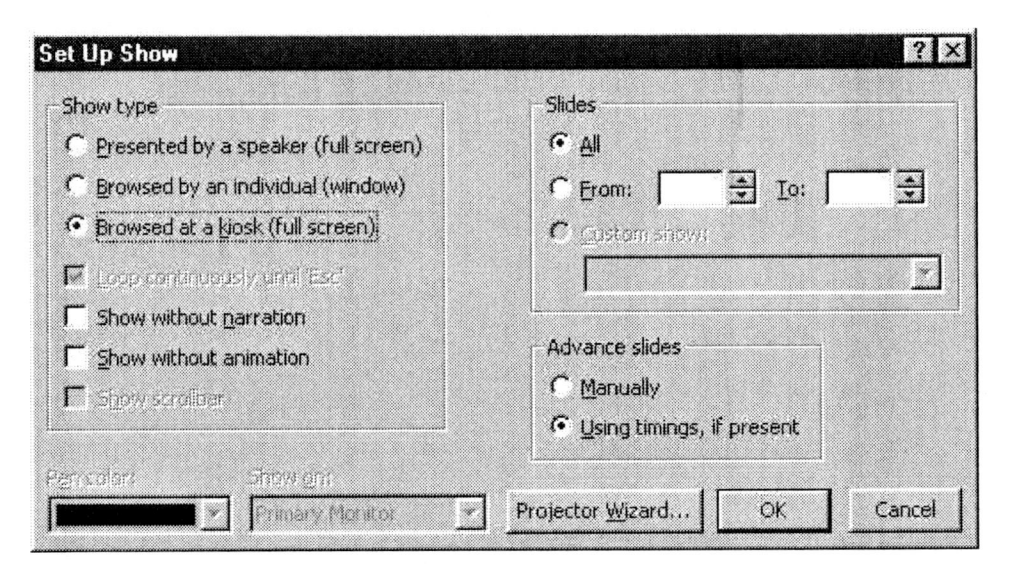

Power Point 2000 users can set the timings of the slides with the Slide Transition dialog box. Click the **Slide Show** menu and choose **Slide Transitions**. In the **Advance** section, uncheck the **On Mouse Click** and click in the **Automatically after** box. Set the time in this box to the number of seconds you think is appropriate for your audience or classroom, and then click **Apply to All**. If the show plays too fast or too slow, you can always return to this dialog box and adjust this setting.

PowerPoint 2002 users should click the **Transition** button in the **Slide Sorter** toolbar while in **Slide Sorter** view. This will bring up the **Slide Transition** task pane. In the **Advance slide section**, uncheck the **On Mouse Click** and click in the **Automatically after** box. Set the time in this box to the number of seconds you think is appropriate for your audience or classroom. If the show plays too fast or too slow, you can always adjust this setting in this task pane.

 ### Trick: Concerned About Time?

If you are concerned about the amount of time that your students need to view slides in a presentation that runs automatically, then teach them to control the advancement of slides by clicking the mouse. In the **Slide Transition** dialog box or the **Slide Transition** task pane's **Advance Slide** area, make sure **On Mouse Click** is selected.

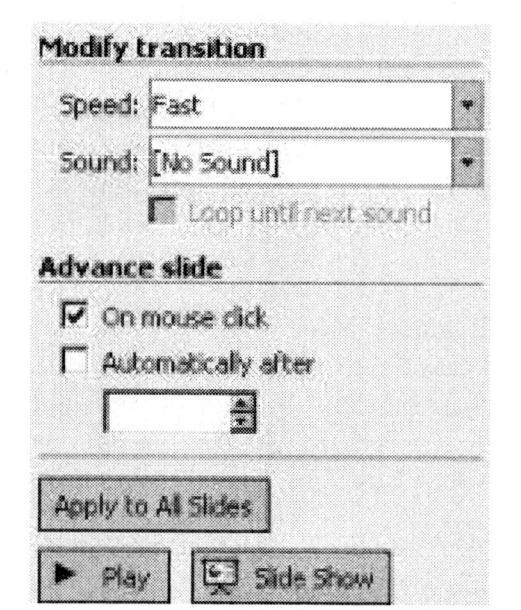

 ### Tip: Rehearse Timings

To accurately set timings for slide shows that advance automatically, click the **Slide Show** menu and choose **Rehearse Timings**. A special floating toolbar will appear that displays the elapsed time. When you think enough time has passed, press the **Spacebar** or the **Page Down** key to move to the next slide. When you reach the end, you will be asked if you want to keep the slide timings for this show. Choose **Yes** to keep the timings.

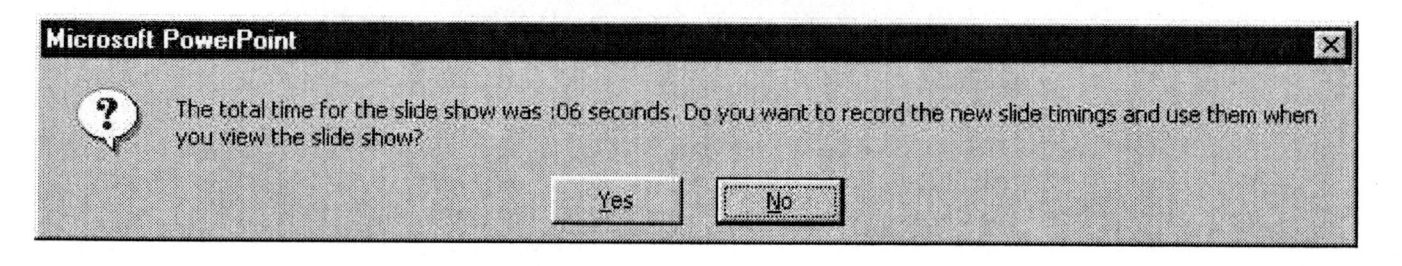

 ### Trick: Double-Click Slide Shows

If you would like your students to run slide shows without having to locate and launch *PowerPoint*, and without having to deal with the *PowerPoint* interface, try saving your *PowerPoint* presentation in a special "show" format. First, just to be safe, save your presentation as you normally do. Then, click the **File** menu and choose **Save As**. In the **Save as Type** drop-down box, choose *PowerPoint* **Show (*pps)**. Give this file a name that is different from your regular *PowerPoint* presentation so you'll be able to tell them apart. Click **Save**. Now your students can simply select this file to automatically run the show.

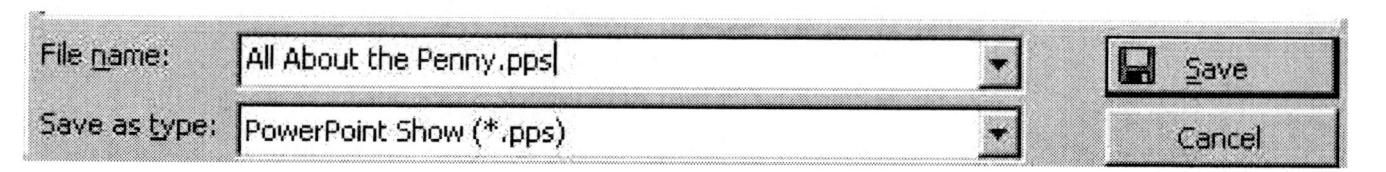

Special Project: Create Instruction Manuals

Share your knowledge with others by creating instruction manuals on *PowerPoint* slides that can be used next to the computer. These instruction manuals can also be used on professional development days when instruction time must be quick and to the point. Finally, students will enjoy creating instruction manuals for special projects or to peer-teach a technology task to others in the classroom. (Thanks to Kathy Schrock for this terrific use of *PowerPoint*!)

Begin by taking screen shots of the particular topics that you would like to teach in a workshop or class. Save these in a graphic format that *PowerPoint* can read, such as JPEG, GIF, or TIFF. Remember that you can scan items or take digital photos and use these too. Put all your items in a folder somewhere on your computer for easy insertion into *PowerPoint*. If you are creating photocopies of your instruction manuals, it might be useful to convert the saved images to grayscale.

Start a blank *PowerPoint* presentation, name it, and save it. On the first two slides, create the introduction to your manual. Be sure to include your name and e-mail address in case your readers have questions later on when they are working on their own. On the third slide, create the written instructions for the first step. Place a screen shot on the fourth slide using the drawing tools in *PowerPoint* to create directional arrows or circles around particular points. Continue in this manner until you have completed the instruction, saving your work as you progress. Don't bother with transitions or animations at this point.

Test your presentation twice, once by viewing it yourself and then again with a colleague or student to see if they can understand the steps in your instruction. Next, create your handout. From the **File** menu, choose **Print**. In the **Print What** section, choose **Handouts**. Set **4** or **6** slides per page and print them out.

**Learning to Play
Audio Tracks
for a PowerPoint
Presentation**

by
Midge Frazel
midgef@midgefrazel.net
http://www.midgefrazel.com

Preparing the Audio CD

- Decide on a CD track to use
- Insert the Audio CD
- Insert the CD icon
- Customize the Sound

Insert the Track

- From the Insert menu, click Movies and Sounds Choose Play CD Audio track
  - —PowerPoint 2000's "Sound Dialog" box appears
  - —"Advanced Sound" Dialogue Box appears

Play the Audio CD

Be sure the CD is in the CD drive
or
Play the audio files stored on your hard drive

Special Project: Photo Album

 ## Idea: Create a Photo Album

Windows users of *PowerPoint 2000* and 2002 can quickly create photo albums of digital images, scanned photos, documents or drawings, or other graphics in a snap using a special feature called Photo Album. The process and the resulting presentation are different for each application so read the section for the version you are using.

 ## Trick: *PowerPoint 2000* Photo Albums

Creating photo albums with *PowerPoint 2000* requires a special add-in wizard which you must download from the Internet. Once installed, you will be able to make these exciting presentations in *PowerPoint 2000*.

Step One: Download and Install

Download the **Photo Album Add-in Program** from **Microsoft's Office Download Center** on the Internet. Save it to the Desktop. Exit your browser and double-click on the file (**album.exe**) to install it.

Step Two: Gather Your Images

Place your digital images in a folder on your desktop. If you are using images directly from a camera or scanner, have them handy. The more organized you are, the faster this process will be.

Step Three: Finding the Wizard

Start *PowerPoint 2000*. At the **New Slide** dialog box, click **Cancel**. From the **File** menu, choose **New**. From the **General** tab, click **Photo Album (photoalbum.pwz)** and then click **OK**. This opens the Photo Album dialog box.

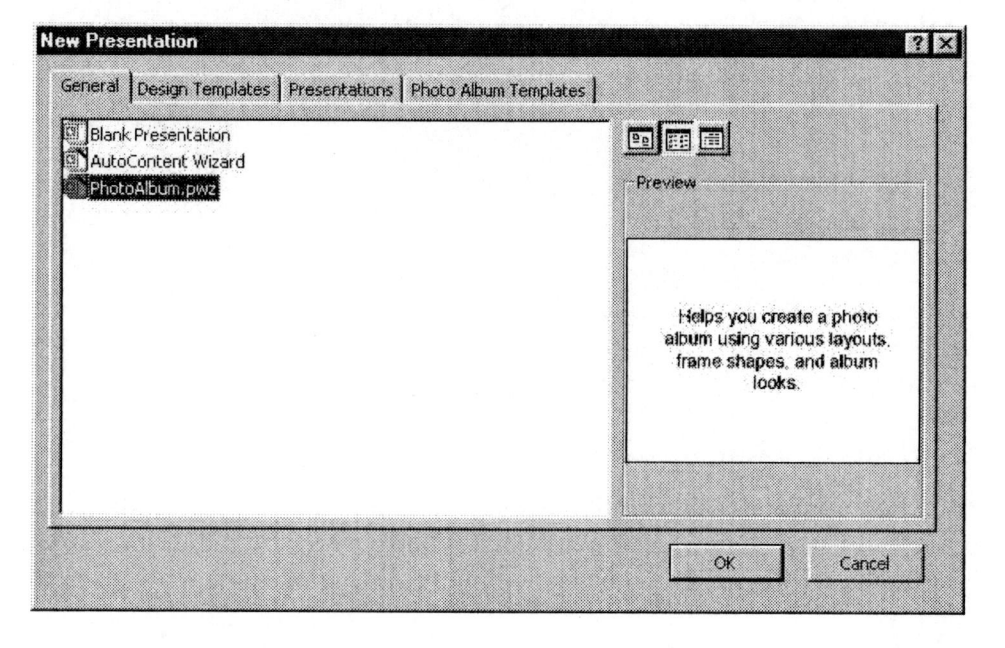

Step Four: Add Images but don't click Create!

In the **Album content** area, click the **File/Disk** button. Navigate to the location where you saved the images. Use **Ctrl-click** to select multiple files (non-contiguous). Use **Shift-click** to select a range. When they are selected, click the **Insert** button. Repeat this process to add images from other folders. Add images from a TWAIN compatible scanner or a directly-connected digital camera by clicking the **Scanner/Camera** button. Do NOT click the Create button until you have completely finished adding and manipulating images.

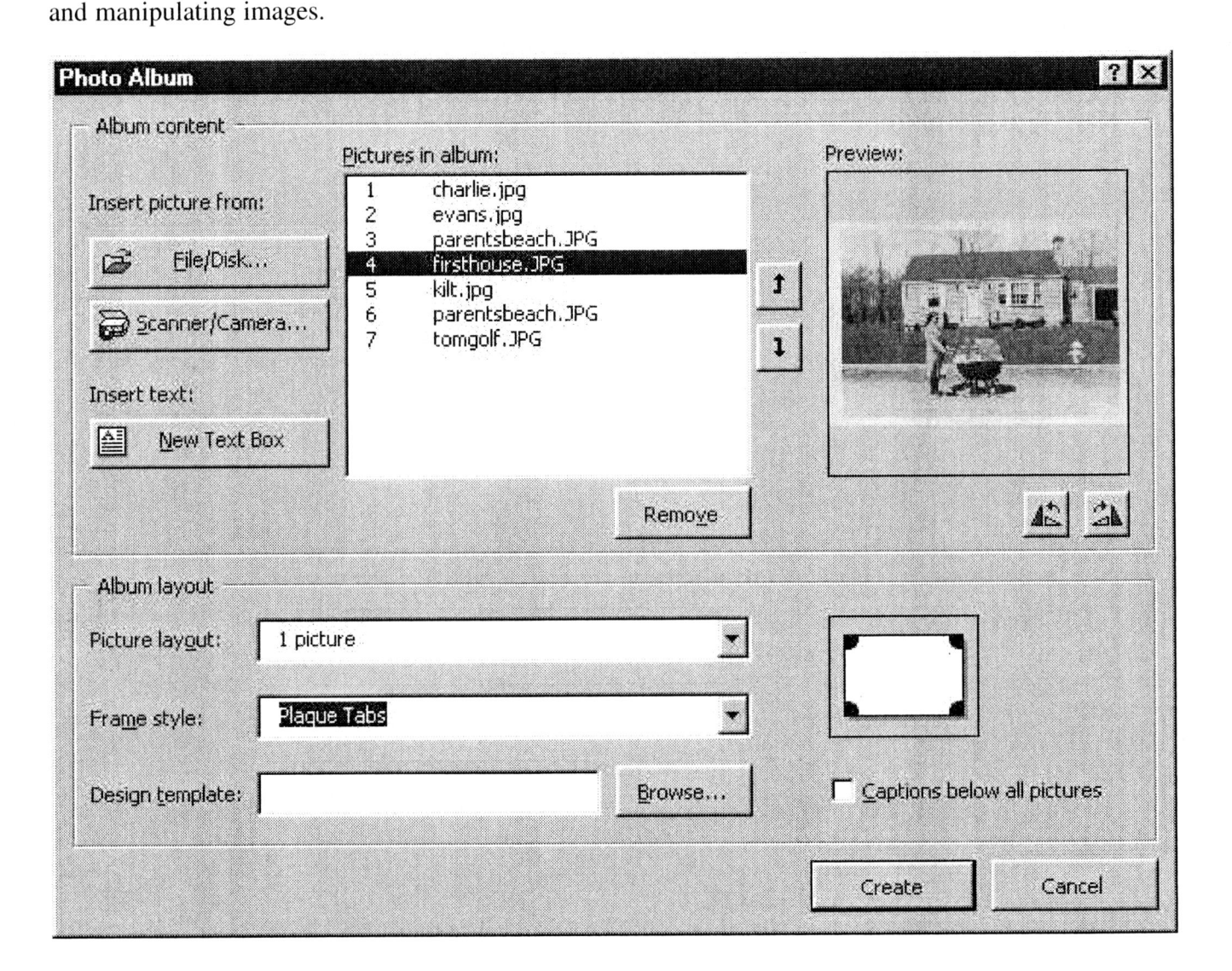

Step Five: Manipulate Images

Click on an image name to select and preview it. With it selected, move it up or down in the list using the move buttons. To remove a photo, select it, and click the **Remove** button. To rotate a photo, select it, then click the **Rotate Right** or **Rotate Left** button.

Step Six: Add Text Boxes

Click the **Text Box** button to add a slide with a blank text box. You will type in the text box later. Click the **Remove** button to remove an unwanted text box. Text boxes are about the same size as an image and take the place of one of the images on pages with multi-image placement.

Step Seven: Set Album Styles

In the **Album layout** section, choose a picture layout. To display your images one-per-slide at the largest size possible, choose **Fit to Slide**. The other choices, including 1 slide, are best for applying a Frame Style to each photo. You can choose to have one, two, or four images per slide or one, two, or four images per slide with a title placeholder. These Frame Styles are special borders applied around the perimeter of the image. You can pick only one of eight Frame Styles, and the one you choose will be applied to all the images in this album. You can also use a Photo Album Design template for a background behind the slides. This background can be any of the design templates you prefer to use in *PowerPoint*. Note that the Fit to Slide Picture layout choice fills the screen, so no design template can be applied.

Step Eight: Click Create!

When you have added all the images, put them in the right order, removed those that don't belong, added text boxes, and added options from the Album styles section, then you can click **Create**. Read the warning message and click **OK**.

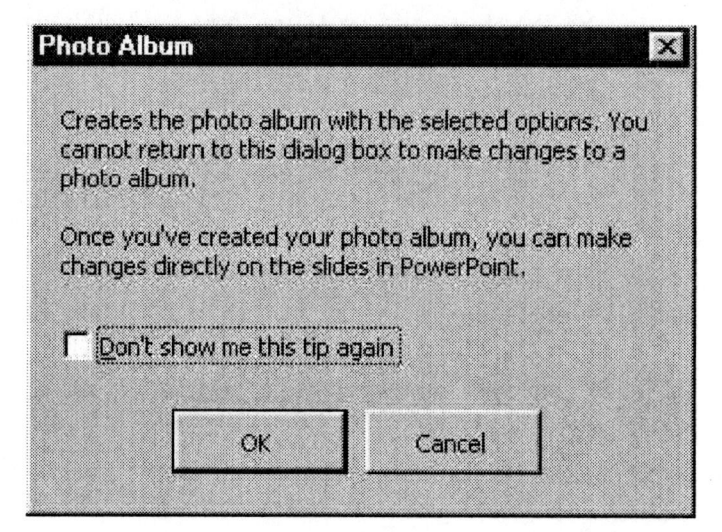

Step Nine: The Photo Album

Your photos will be placed in a presentation that you can work on in *PowerPoint*. Remember to name and save the presentation before you begin working on it. You will not be able to add additional images at this point (with the multi-layout or frame styles applied), but you can add transitions, sounds, and audio CD tracks as you would with any other presentation.

 ## Trick: PowerPoint 2002 Photo Albums

Step One: Gather Your Images

Place your digital images in a folder on your desktop. If you are using images directly from a camera or scanner, have them handy. The more organized you are, the faster this process will be.

Step Two: Start a Photo Album

Start a new presentation with a blank slide. Click the **Insert** menu, choose **Picture**, and then select **New Photo Album**.

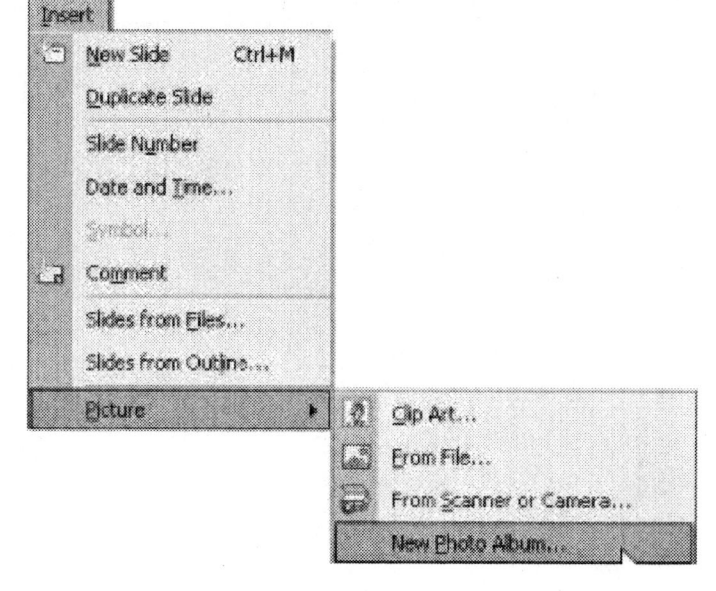

Step Three: Adding Images with The Photo Album dialog box

In the **Album** content area, click the **File/Disk** button. Navigate to the location where you saved the images. Use **Ctrl-click** to select multiple files (non-contiguous). Use **Shift-click** to select a range. When they are selected, click the **Insert** button. Repeat this process to add images from other folders. Add images from a TWAIN compatible scanner or a directly-connected digital camera by clicking the **Scanner/Camera** button.

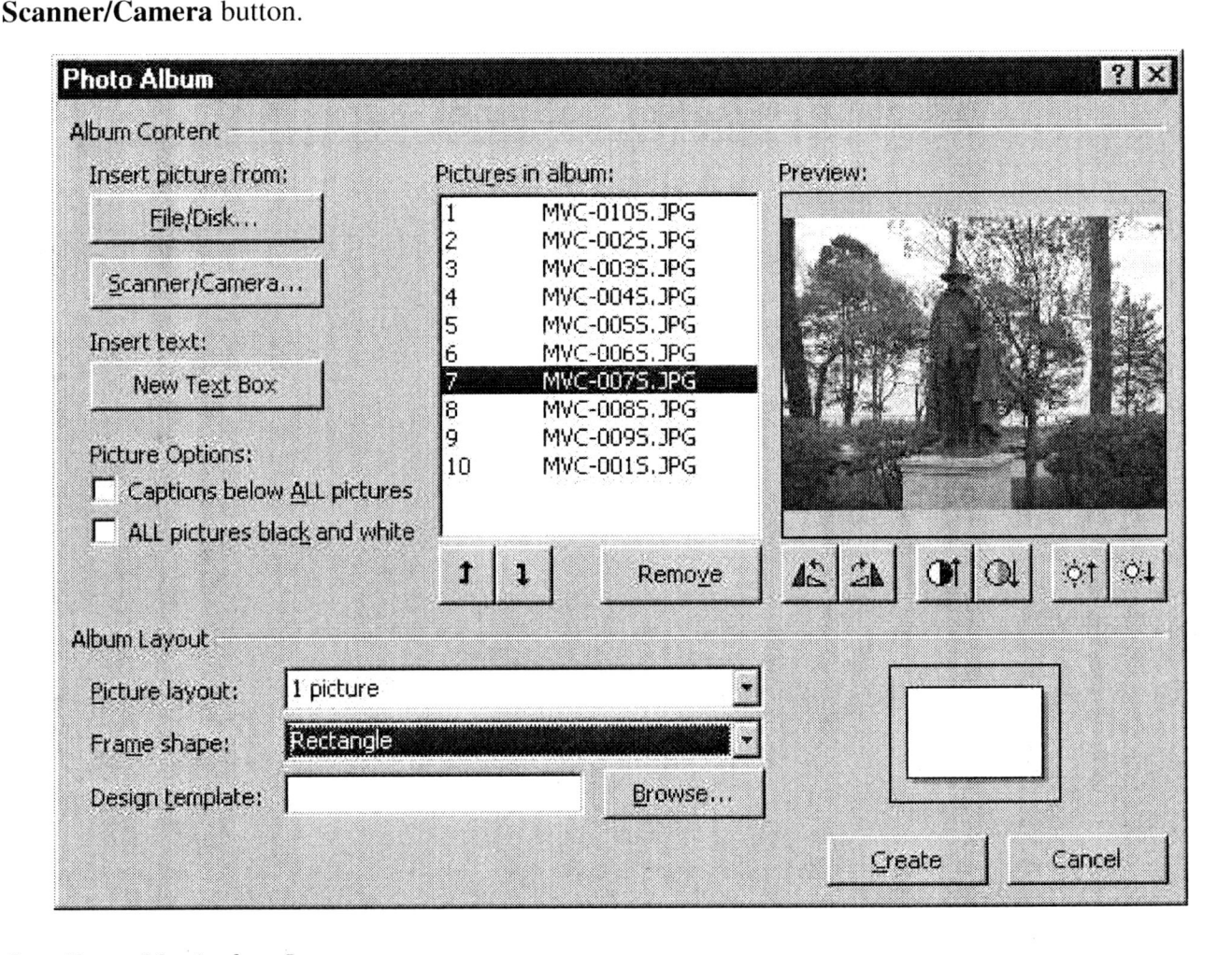

Step Four: Manipulate Images

Click on an image name to select and preview it. With it selected, move it up or down in the list with the move buttons. To remove a photo, select it, and click the **Remove** button. To rotate a photo, select it, then click the **Rotate Right** or **Rotate Left** button. Adjust the brightness and contrast of each image with the **Brightness** and **Contrast** buttons.

Step Five: Add Text Boxes

Click the **Text Box** button to add a slide with a blank text box. You will type in the text box later in *PowerPoint*. Click the **Remove** button to remove an unwanted text box. Text boxes are about the same size as an image and take the place of one of the images on pages with multi-image placement. Making the images black and white and adding captions below each picture are two picture options available with some Picture layouts.

Step Six: Set Album Styles

In the **Album layout** section, choose a picture layout. To display your images one-per-slide at the largest size possible, choose **Fit to Slide**. The other choices, including 1 slide, are best for applying a Frame Style to each photo. You can choose to put one, two, or four images per slide or one, two, or four images per slide with a title placeholder. These Frame Styles are special borders applied around the perimeter of the image. You can pick only one of eight Frame Styles. The style you choose will be applied to all the images in this album. You can also use a Photo Album Design template for a background behind the slides. This background can be any of the design templates you prefer to use in *PowerPoint*. Note that the Fit to Slide Picture layout choice fills the screen and no design template can be applied.

Step Seven: Create the Album

When you are finished with the options in the Photo Album dialog box, click the **Create** button. The resulting album will open in *PowerPoint*. Now you can add your finishing touches. If you want to add more images, click the **Format** menu and choose **Photo Album**. Be sure to read the message at the bottom of this dialog box before clicking the **Update** button.

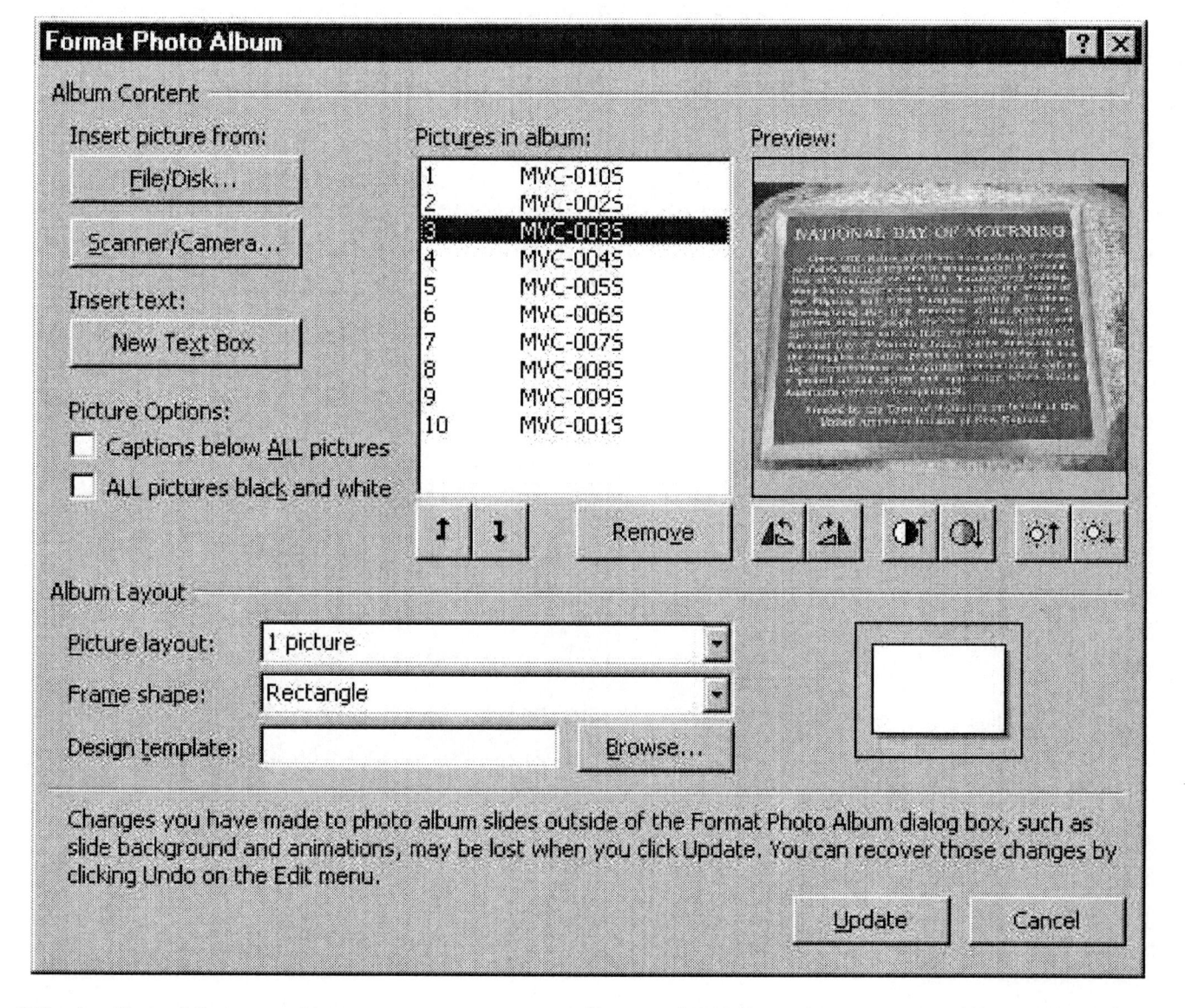

Notes